Woodworking
for Kids

Woodworking for Kids

40 Fabulous, Fun & Useful Things for Kids to Make

■■■■■■■

Kevin McGuire

A Sterling/Lark Book

Sterling Publishing Co., Inc.   New York

Editor: Chris Rich

Art Director: Chris Colando

Production: Elaine Thompson, Chris Colando, Charlie Covington

Photography: Evan Bracken

Illustrations: Kevin Maguire

Library of Congress Cataloging-in-Publication Data
McGuire, Kevin, 1952-
    Woodworking for kids : 40 fabulous, fun, and useful things
for kids to make / by Kevin McGuire.
      p.   cm.
    "A Sterling/Lark book."
    Includes index.
    Summary: Introduces the tools and techniques of woodworking
and provides instructions for various projects.
    ISBN 0-8069-0429-1
    1. Woodwork--Juvenile literature.   [1. Woodwork.
  2. Handicraft.]
  I. Title
  TT185.W6594   1993
  684'.08--dc20   93-20489
                                      CIP
                                      AC

10 9 8 7

A Sterling/Lark Book

First paperback edition published in 1994 by
Sterling Publishing Company, Inc.
387 Park Avenue South, New York, N.Y. 10016

Produced and © 1993 by Altamont Press, Inc.
67 Broadway Asheville, NC 28801

Distributed in Canada by Sterling Publishing
⁒ Canadian Manda Group, P.O. Box 920, Station U
Toronto, Ontario, Canada M8Z 5P9
Distributed in Great Britain and Europe by Chrysalis Books
64 Brewery Road, London N7 9NT, England
Distributed in Australia by Capricorn Link (Australia) Pty Ltd.
P. O. Box 704, Windsor, NSW 2756 Australia

Every effort has been made to ensure that all the information in this book is
accurate. However, due to differing conditions, tools, and individual skills,
the publisher cannot be responsible for any injuries, losses, and other
damages which may result from the use of the information in this book.

Sterling ISBN 0-8069-0429-1 Trade
                0-8069-0430-5 Paper

Contents

Introduction

YOU CAN BUILD IT!

Not the whole forest—just one leaf.
　　　　　　　　—*P.L. Travers*

When the author of *Mary Poppins* wrote this line, she could have been talking to a young woodworker just like you. Let's think about it. If you tried to picture in your mind a forest that you'd only walked through once, you'd have an awfully hard time, wouldn't you? And if you tried to build a six-story building with tools you'd never used before, the building might collapse! But you *can* get to know a forest, and you *can* become a top-notch woodworker. How? The secret is simple: "Just one leaf."

You can get to know a forest, but only if you start by getting to know the leaves and trees in it. In the same way, you can become a great woodworker by getting to know your tools and materials before you head straight for the most complicated project you can think of. Begin with the basics; read the first two parts of this book. Then get some practice by making the workshop projects in "Part Three." Once you've completed these five useful projects, you'll be ready to move on to the building adventures in "Part Four."

A small stack of boards, some nails, and a little glue can become just about anything you want— your own wooden tool box, for a start. Yes, the tool box is one of the first projects in this book, and you can build it. What about a rope ladder to hang in a backyard tree, a pair of stilts, or a puppet theater? All these sensational projects (and 36 more) are included, and they're yours for the building. Some are simple, and others are more challenging, but every one of them is designed to help your woodworking skills to grow. And once you've mastered basic woodworking skills, there won't be any stopping you. Before long, you'll be dreaming up the "impossible" and building it. In the meantime, have fun!

HOW TO USE THIS BOOK

Anyone can build with wood. You don't have to be an adult to use woodworking tools. In fact, you don't have to be anything except

Building Dreams

Wood, the amazing forest material that we use every day and see around us everywhere, is full of magic. People have used it for centuries to build almost anything you can imagine. Did you know, for instance, that the Spruce Goose—a giant airplane with the widest wingspan ever built—had a body made entirely of wood? Or that the body of the first motorcycle, built in Germany in 1885, had many wooden parts—including its wheels? Wood is perfect for building dreams! Now that plastics and other man-made materials are everywhere, we still use wood for its great strength and beauty—and for the excitement of working with this wonderful material. You'll soon find that it's the friendliest, most fascinating material you've ever used.

First motorcycle ever made, built with wooden parts. *Riding Car* (Daimler-Benz), 1885. Courtesy German Information Center, New York.

enthusiastic, curious, and big enough to hold a hammer or saw! With the help of this book (and now and then, an adult friend), you'll soon be putting together your own great-looking projects.

Begin by reading the section after this one—"Working Together." It will explain when, why, and how adults can help you. Then move on to "Part One: Getting Started." With its help, you'll discover

◆ where wood comes from and how it's turned into boards

◆ the many kinds and sizes of wood that you can get at your local lumberyard

◆ which tools and materials you'll need to build your first projects

◆ how to set up your workshop and how to work safely

Once you have your tool kit, some boards, and some hardware, turn to "Part Two: Tools and Techniques." In it, you'll find everything you need to know about your tools and materials, including how to hammer a nail, how to square a board, and much more. Browse through the helpful hints and photographs. Later, whenever you or your adult helper have questions, you can come back to this part and use it as a reference. (The "Ready Reference" section at the very end of this book will tell you exactly how the information in "Part Two" is organized.)

"Part Three: Building Five Basic Tools" is especially important, so don't skip it! You'll not only be making five terrific tools for your own workshop, but you'll also be practicing the basic techniques that you'll use when you build the projects in "Part Four." As you construct your own bench hook, for example, you'll get to know your tape measure, square, and handsaw by squaring and sawing a board, and as you make the bit caddy, you'll learn how to cut out a curved shape with your coping saw.

After you've built these handy workshop helpers, you'll be ready to roll. In "Part Four: Pick Your Projects!" you'll discover some wonderful things to build, and they're all arranged in groups that will make it easy for you to choose your favorites.

Each project's *skill level* is identified with a symbol so that you can tell at a glance whether you want to tackle it. When you see a ◆❶, you can be sure that the project is fairly easy. A ◆❷ tells you that the project is more challenging. And

projects identified with a ◆❸ are the most challenging of all. Choose a skill level that's comfortable for you. When it begins to feel too easy, just move on to more complicated projects. Your adult guide can help you decide when to graduate to a higher level.

Before you build a project, read the lists that come with it. The *Materials* list will tell you exactly what you'll need: how much lumber, what kind of hardware, and what type of finishing materials, for example. The *Cut List* will describe each piece of lumber that you'll need to cut and will give you its dimensions. The *Tools* list will tell you which tools you'll need.

Next, read through the project's instructions. As you do, imagine yourself taking each step before you actually pick up your tools. Then, if you have any questions about tools, techniques, or materials, you can get the answers ahead of time instead of having to stop while you're building. If new questions come up while you're

Woodworking for Young People with Special Needs

All young woodworkers can experience the rewards of completing a project and the real pleasure of saying, "I built it!" Young people with special needs are no exception. For their adult helpers, who will want to be especially involved in the building process, following are a few suggestions:

♦ Adapt the projects when necessary. Use latex paints instead of oil-based finishes, for example, or simplify patterns.

♦ Assist the physically disabled with more intricate techniques. When challenge ends and frustration begins, offer a guiding hand.

♦ Explain each step of the construction process carefully, especially when the young woodworker finds reading difficult.

♦ Divide the construction procedures into smaller segments.

♦ Illustrate steps with hand-sketched drawings.

♦ Model a project for the young builder by making an identical project at the same time.

working on a project (and they probably will, no matter how many you've thought of beforehand), take the time to find the answers. When you can't find an answer in this book, ask your adult helper; that's what he or she is there for!

When you're comfortable using your woodworking tools, and when you know how to use them safely, there won't be any limits to what you can build!

WORKING TOGETHER

Your most important woodworking tool is an adult who can give you a hand. That's right! Think about it for a minute. Your other tools are fun to use, but they're mighty quiet. They can't give you

tips on how to saw a board the easy way or how to hold a rasp just right. And friends your own age may be terrific work-mates, but they'll probably have as many questions about woodworking as you do. This book will give you lots of ideas and plans for building, but the one tool you really need is an older helper, who will listen, give you a hand, and enjoy working at your side as you learn about building.

Have your helper read the first two parts of this book. Then compare notes. What tools do you have already? Where would you like to set up your workshop? Make a list of what you need, including tools that you don't have and materials for the first

couple of projects. Visit your local lumberyard or building supply store—together. Ask questions! You're sure to find people who are willing to answer them for you.

After you've carted your purchases back to your workshop, read your project instructions carefully, and then have your helper be your guide as you use each new tool and material. If you need help holding your saw at the right angle or clamping boards together, say so. Talk over any problems you're having; together you can find a solution. You'll have your first project assembled in no time at all, and what a fine moment that will be. Get friends and other family members involved, too. After all, woodworking is for everyone!

Part One: Getting Started

GIFT FROM THE FOREST

Wood is wonderful. Just try to imagine what a cold and colorless place our world would be without it—a lifeless world of steel, glass, and plastic. Look around the room you're in this very moment; you're bound to see things around you that are made of wood. Where does all this wood come from?

All wood begins as a living, growing tree. The tree's thirsty roots tug water and food from the earth below, and its fluttering crown of leaves drinks bright sunlight from

the sky above. Look carefully at any piece of wood: a clean board fresh from the lumberyard, a rough piece of firewood, or a cracked and worn table top. In that wood, you can read the story of how it once grew, how it stretched, and how it spread its limbs. Listen closely enough, and you can almost hear the echoes of birds who once sang and nested high in those branches.

Notice the wood's *grain*—the thin, wavy lines running along the wood, generally in one direction. Grain is what remains of the tiny "rivers" that used to carry moisture and nutrients up the tree's long trunk to its leafy heights. Grain can point you toward each part of a board. It flows along the *faces* and *edges* of a board, and it stops at the *ends.* Because no two boards ever have exactly the same pattern of grain, each of your projects will have a special beauty.

Parts of a Board

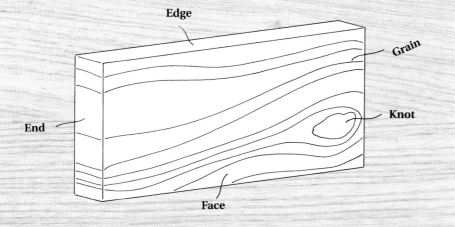

Edge

Grain

End

Knot

Face

Most boards used for building are made up of three parts: edges, faces, and ends. Knowing the names for these parts will help you to understand how a project fits together, and using these names will help you to explain the project to your helpers. When you read a project's instructions, pay close attention to these three words; they'll guide you as you work.

Look at the end of a board. The alternating light and dark layers that you see are the soft, fast-growing early wood of spring and the harder, slower-growing late wood of summer. Each pair of layers represents a year's growth, and the pattern of layers gives a visible history of the tree's lifetime. *Knots* in a piece of wood (the dark, round spots where smaller limbs joined the tree trunk) and other markings give clues about how the wood grew; they make each piece of wood unique.

Not all wood is the same. Different trees produce different kinds of wood which vary in color, weight, hardness, and other qualities. More than twenty thousand types of trees are known throughout the world, and others await discovery even today.

FROM FOREST TO LUMBERYARD

Lumber, the wood we use for building, begins as logs harvested from forests or from giant plantations where fields are planted with only one type of tree. These logs are delivered to *mills,* where they're skinned of their bark, sawn into rough boards, and then dried out in enormous heated ovens called *kilns* (pronounced "kills"). Next, the boards are *dressed* (smoothed with large knives), bundled, and delivered to the lumberyard.

Have you ever heard the word *nominal?* It means "in name only." The wood that you buy at the lumberyard is sorted, named, and sold by its nominal size—a size that isn't accurate! It's a size in name only. Most lumber is actually smaller than its name suggests—not as thick and not as wide. In the old days, a 1 x 4 *was* exactly 1" x 4", but nowadays, its *actual* (or real) size is only about 3/4" thick x 3-1/2" wide. The chart on this page shows you the difference between nominal and actual sizes for common lumber.

Even the actual sizes listed aren't always exact because every board expands or contracts, depending on how wet or dry the air around it is. Always measure the width and thickness of each board before you pick up your saw!

There's one measurement you can depend on—a board's length. When you buy a 1 x 4 x 8' board, that last measurement (the length) will be pretty accurate. A 1 x 4 x 8' board is never shorter than eight feet. A 2 x 4 x 12' board is always at least twelve feet long. In fact, the boards you buy may even be a little bit longer than you need.

Get to know the different sizes of lumber so that you won't waste money and materials by getting lumber that's the wrong size for your project. The Materials list in

Woodworking Symbols

" = inch or inches

' = foot or feet

x = by

Example: A 3/4" x 1-1/12" x 12' board is three-quarters of an inch thick by one and one-half inches wide by twelve feet long.

Nominal Size	Actual Size
1 x 2	3/4" x 1-1/2"
1 x 4	3/4" x 3-1/2"
1 x 6	3/4" x 5-1/2"
1 x 8	3/4" x 7-1/4"
1 x 10	3/4" x 9-1/4"
1 x 12	3/4" x 11-1/4"
2 x 2	1-1/2" x 1-1/2"
2 x 4	1-1/2" x 3-1/2"
2 x 6	1-1/2" x 5-1/2"

each project will tell you exactly what size lumber you need.

Lumber is also sorted by its *grade*, which depends on how many knots and other kinds of defects it has in it. Your projects will look better and will be easier to build if you buy one of the better grades (such as *Clear*, which has no knots). Better grades are more expensive, though, so if you don't have extra dollars to spend on high-grade lumber, don't worry. Just buy the best grade that you can afford.

For most of the projects in this book, you'll be using *pine* lumber. It's a light-colored, lightweight, fairly strong wood, which makes it ideal for a wide range of projects—from bird boxes to bull-roarers. You may use some *spruce* lumber, too, in projects where thicker pieces are required. Use whatever lumber fits the sizes listed in your project's Materials list and is available in your hometown.

While many logs are sawn and dressed into lumber for building, others are peeled like giant potatoes into thin slices. These slices

Help! It's Alive!

Well, not really, but wood *does* move, even if it's no longer alive. Why? Because water passes back and forth between the wood and the air around it. When wood absorbs moisture, it swells. When it loses moisture, it shrinks. And when one part of a board absorbs or loses moisture more rapidly than another, the board curls (or, as a woodworker would say, *warps* or *bows*).

Nothing can stop wood from moving. Believe it or not, every board in your home is moving at this very moment! There are a couple of tricks you can use to protect your finished projects from warping and bowing, though. One is to use screws instead of nails. Screws are stronger and help keep wide boards flat. The other is to apply finishes such as varnish or paint; these act like armor to protect water from moving in and out of the wood too quickly.

are glued together and then trimmed to make large flat sheets of *plywood.* You'll be using plywood when you need to cover a large area, such as the top of the workbench project. Like lumber, plywood comes in several grades. *Fir paint-grade* plywood has at least one smooth surface that is free from defects. You can probably have someone at the lumberyard saw the 4' x 8' sheet into the smaller pieces that you need. This will save you time later (plywood is difficult to cut) and will also make it much easier to carry the plywood home. Make sure to get plywood that is the right thickness for your project: 1/4", 3/8", 1/2", or whatever. Save any extra pieces for future projects.

Special kinds of wood that you'll find at the lumberyard include *dowels* (round poles) and *lattice* (thin strips). *Balsa wood,* which you'll find at your local hobby shop or crafts store, is a very lightweight wood. It's used to build model airplanes and for other craft projects.

With this book and your tape measure, visit your lumberyard or building supply store, and ask to see their lumber. You'll notice right away that different sizes of wood are stacked separately. If you have questions or can't find the material you need, show this book—and the project instructions for what you want to build— to someone who works at the lumberyard. He or she will give you a hand. All that wood in the store may confuse you at first, but you'll feel right at home before long.

SETTING UP SHOP

The more you work with wood, the larger your collection of tools and supplies will grow. You don't need a fancy workshop or hundreds of tools to begin building these projects, however. Remember: "Just one leaf." Two shopping lists follow. One includes every tool in the Even-Dozen Tool Kit, and one lists basic materials.

The Even-Dozen Tool Kit

Pencil

Tape measure, 8'-long

Try square

C-clamp (6"), one or two

Claw hammer, 13- or 16-ounce

Handsaw (crosscut), total length 20" or less

Twist drill, with 1/8" and 5/32" bits

Screwdriver, No. 2 Phillips

Screwdriver, No. 2 flat-bladed

Coping saw, with a few replaceable blades

Rasp (half-round)

Brace and bit, with 1/4", 3/8", 1/2", 3/4" and 1" bits

Basic Materials

Nails, one pound each of 3d, 4d, and 6d finishing; one dozen each of 8d and 16d common; one box of No. 17 x 3/4" brads

Flathead wood screws (Phillips), one dozen No. 10 x 1-1/2"

Yellow carpenter's glue or white glue, 8-ounce bottle

Sandpaper (100-grit and 50-grit garnet), several sheets of each

Paper dust-masks, several

Latex high-gloss enamel paint, half-pints in your favorite colors

Oil-based stain and varnish, one half-pint or pint of each

Mineral spirits or turpentine, one quart of either

Paintbrushes, 1" flat, 1/2" flat, and detail

Rags and newspapers

Sticks for stirring

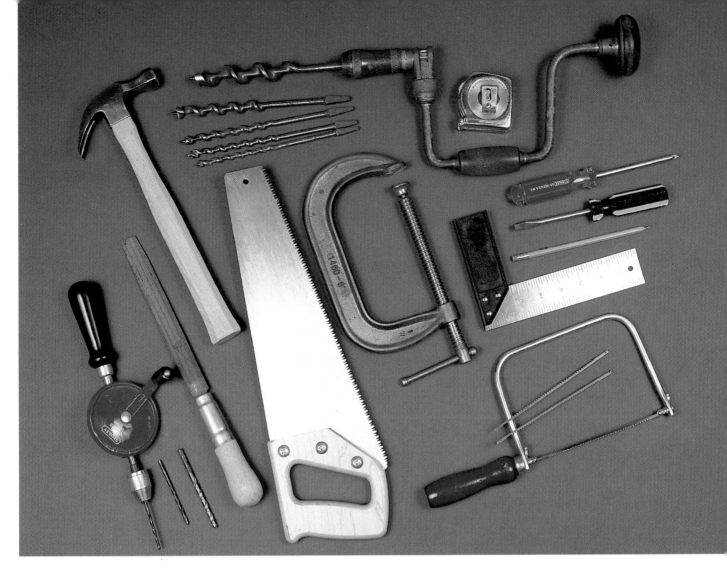
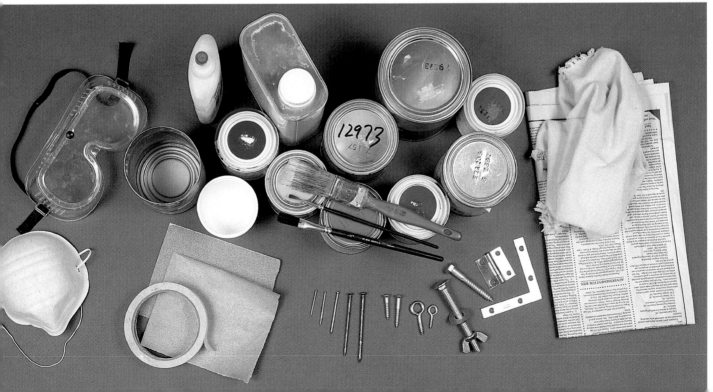

Complete descriptions of these tools and materials are given in "Part Two." You might want to read these before you go shopping so that you'll know more about what you're looking for!

Start by purchasing as many of the listed tools as you can afford, and buy the best. Cheap tools aren't any fun to use. They don't work very well, they don't last very long, and they don't help you to do your very best work. If you use a dull, bent saw, for instance, you'll never get a really straight cut.

Good tools can be expensive, so consider getting only the first six on the list; you'll need them to build the very first project. Then add tools gradually until your kit is complete. Look for used tools at yard sales and at antique stores, too, but always try these out before you buy them. Of course, if someone in your home already has the tools, you can save some money by sharing them. Owning your own tool kit, however, will encourage you to use it often and to care for it well.

Once you've got a few tools, buy some basic supplies. Stock your workshop with nails, screws, glue, sandpaper, and dust masks. These materials will get you off to a great start and can all be purchased at a lumberyard or hardware store. Add paints, stains, varnishes, and other finishing materials as you need them.

Some projects, such as the workbench, require special hardware, so always check your project's Materials list before you go shopping. Check that same list to find out what lumber you'll need to get, too. To cut down on expenses, keep leftover pieces of wood in your scrap bin, and use these small pieces on other projects.

The Scrap Bin

Forests are precious to us for many reasons; you can help to protect them by not wasting wood. Store your leftover wood in a large cardboard box or a similar bin, and use these scraps when you need a small piece of wood for another project. It's much easier to go to that bin than to go to the lumberyard, and it's much easier on our forests, too!

KEEPING IT SAFE

Building safely is the only way to go. Why? Because all the fun disappears when someone gets hurt. Think of your tools as friends who treat you just as well as you treat them. Give them the respect they deserve, and they'll do wonderful things for you!

Here are three tips to keep you building safely:

Take Your Time

The whole idea is to have a good time, right? Building *is* fun, too, unless you're rushing to slap a project together. When you're tired and confused and can't remember what fits where, stop, take a deep breath, and remind yourself to relax! Take a break, go for a walk, and dream about how good that finished project will look if you build it slowly and carefully. When you're ready to start work again, you'll feel much better, and you'll do much better work.

Pay Attention to Your Work

Pay close attention while you work. Tools can be good friends, but when you don't handle them properly, they can hurt you. *Horseplay* (dropping tools and tossing them around) is a good way to turn your tools into enemies. If you find that your attention is drifting away from what you're doing, put everything away, and call it a day.

Ask an Adult for Help

When you're uncomfortable using a tool or when you can't understand your project's instructions, go ahead and ask an adult to give you a hand. Two heads are almost always better than one, and four hands can do a lot more than two. Working together with someone older than you are doesn't mean that the

project isn't yours anymore. Just think of that adult as someone who can double the fun you have building your project—someone who can share your excitement. And keep asking questions until you understand what you're doing.

Common Sense Safety Rules

A safe workshop area will help you to build your best work. Whether you set up your shop indoors or outdoors, get some help arranging it so that you have enough room to move boards around and enough light to see your work clearly. Your work surface should be about 30" high, sturdy, and large enough to support the tools and lumber that you're using. (The workbench project in this book is ideal.) Pick up any scrap wood off the floor so that you won't trip on it, and never leave a board that has sharp nails in it lying on the floor—even for a moment.

◆ If you have long hair, tie it up or wear a cap so that it won't catch in your tools. Like long hair, loose clothing can also catch on sharp tool edges. Roll up your sleeves, and hang your scarf on a peg before you begin!

◆ Flying nails can hurt your eyes, so wear a pair of *clear plastic goggles* whenever you pick up a hammer. You can purchase these sight-savers at your building supply store.

◆ Oil-based stains and varnishes, mineral spirits, and turpentine give off poisonous and flammable fumes, so when the weather's good, do your finishing work outdoors. When you have to work indoors, turn on a strong fan, and keep the windows open. And no matter where you work, stay away from any source of heat or open flame.

◆ A *paper dust-mask* will keep sawdust out of your lungs. Get several when you buy your supplies.

◆ Of course, every builder expects a small splinter or scrape now and then, so keep a *first-aid kit* in your shop. And just remember: you can build safely by taking your time, paying attention to your work, and asking an adult for help when you need it.

What About Power Tools?

You've probably seen adults using power tools for woodworking, perhaps in your own home. The small electric motors in these tools move the parts that do the work. In an electric drill, for instance, the motor turns the chuck that holds the drill bit, and it does so much more quickly than you ever could by hand!

Power tools have some real advantages over the hand tools in your Even-Dozen Tool Kit. They allow a builder to make projects quickly. They can take some of the tiring work out of a job. And because a lot of the work is being done by the power tool instead of by the builder, the builder can concentrate on guiding the tool instead of worrying about exerting pressure or turning a gear.

Power tools have some disadvantages, too. They are sometimes too large and heavy for a young builder's hands. They often require an extension cord or a nearby electrical outlet, and they can be very dangerous if they're handled carelessly. While power tools can save a lot of time, keep in mind that the best projects are never built in a hurry! The extra time that hand tools require may help you to think through the construction steps more carefully and may even result in a better-looking completed project.

If you'd like to try using a power tool, first talk it over with your adult helper. Don't ever use one unless your helper is present! For young builders, the most useful power tools are sanders (sometimes called *pad sanders*, for the soft rubber pad that sup-

ports the sandpaper in them) and drills. Try using a rented tool (they're often available by the day at tool rental shops) before you rush out to buy a new one.

For the best results with power tools, always remember that using them requires both your careful attention and the support of an adult helper.

Part Two: Tools & Techniques

In this chapter, you'll find complete explanations of how to use your Even-Dozen Tool Kit and your basic materials. Browse through it before you start your first project, and come back to it every time you have a question. Flip to the "Ready Reference" section at the very back of this book for help finding any information that you need.

USING YOUR MARKING TOOLS

Your marking tools for these projects are a *pencil*, a *tape measure*, and a *try square*. You'll use them to measure, mark, and square your boards before you cut, drill, or fasten them. You already know how to use a pencil! Keep it sharp, and keep an extra pencil handy, too.

Using Your Tape Measure

A tape measure looks like a rolled-up ruler. The coiled *tape*, which unwinds from inside a protective *case*, is marked in feet, inches, and parts of inches. There's a *spring* inside the case, which pulls the tape back inside. And there's a *locking button* on the outside, which you can press to keep the tape extended once you've pulled it out. The *hook* on the case will let you hang your tape measure from your belt or pocket.

You'll use your tape measure to make sure that each piece of wood in your project is the right size. You'll also use it to check the size of your hardware and other materials. Careful measurements are really important. In fact, good woodworkers often say, "Measure

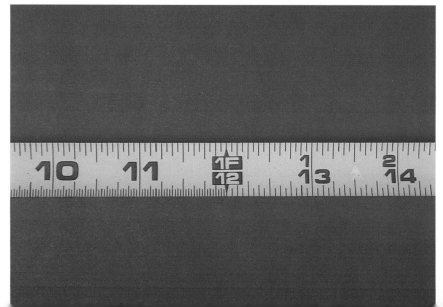

twice, cut once." Why? Because double-checking your measurements and comparing them with those in your project's Cut List will save you from having to re-cut a carelessly measured board!

Outside and Inside Measuring

To measure along or across the *outside* of a board, slip the hook on the tape's end over the board's edge or end. You'll notice that the hook is a little loose. Don't worry; it should be! Next, pull the case so that the tape extends along or across the board. Find the same length on the tape measure as the one given in the project's Cut List, and use your pencil to mark that spot on the board. (Measure all boards before you cut them, too, to make sure that they're long enough to give you all the project pieces that you need.)

When you're measuring from the *inside* end or edge of a piece of wood that already has another piece nailed onto it, push the tape's hook tightly against the joint's corner, and hold it with one finger while you unroll the tape along the board.

Using Your Try Square

The two parts of this L-shaped tool, its *handle* and metal *blade*, are held *square* (at a right angle) to one another by screws. The blade is sometimes marked with inches and parts of inches.

The try square's shape is important, since its main job is to help you check and make right angles. Most of the projects in this book require pieces that fit squarely to one another, so you'll be using this tool a lot! You'll need it

◆ to find out whether or not the end of a board is square (cut at right angles to the board's edge), before you take any measurements from that end

◆ to mark a new end—one that is square—when your try square shows you that a board's end is crooked

◆ to mark a square line at a certain distance from the squared end of a board, one that will guide you when you cut a project piece

◆ to see whether or not two boards are nailed together at a perfect right angle

Checking a Board's End for Square

If you take measurements from the crooked end of a board, the project piece that you cut won't fit squarely with other parts of the project. Before you take any measurements from a board's end, always check to see that the end is square. To do this, hold the inside edge of the try square's handle tightly against one edge of the board, and hook the metal blade over the board's end. If the board's end lines up exactly with the blade's edge, and no space shows between them, the board is square. If the board isn't square, you'll need to square, mark, and cut a new square end.

Squaring a Crooked Board

To square the crooked end of a board, press the edge of the try square's handle tightly against one edge of the board, and let the metal blade lie flat across the

Checking for a Right Angle

After you've nailed two boards together at right angles, use your try square to see if they're square to each other. Fit the try square into the inside corners where the two boards meet. Press the handle against one board, and then check to see whether or not the edge of the blade is tight against the other board. If there's a space between the blade and the board, you'll need to adjust or re-fasten one of the boards until both boards are at right angles before you add other pieces to your project.

When your try square won't fit into the inside corner of your project because the project is too small, you can check for a right angle by holding the try square tightly against the outside corner instead. If there's no space between the try square's edges and the boards, the boards form a right angle.

board's face, about 2" from the crooked end. Use your pencil to draw a line along the blade's edge, from one edge of the board to the other. You'll use this marked line to guide you as you saw off the crooked end.

Marking a Square Line for Sawing

When you need to cut a project piece to a certain length, first make sure that one end of your board is square (and square it if it isn't). Then, measuring from the square end, mark the length of the piece that you want to cut. Next, press the try square's handle against the board's edge, and line up one edge of the blade with the mark you've made. With your pencil, mark a square line across the board's face, and you're ready to cut!

Squaring Across a Wide Board

Most try squares have short blades, about 6" long. To mark a square line across a board that's

wider than 6", first square across as far as you can with your try square and pencil. Then flip the try square to the board's other edge, and line up the blade's edge with the line that you've just marked. Use your pencil to complete that square line across the board.

USING YOUR C-CLAMP

This tool's job is to act like an extra pair of hands. It's used to grip one or more pieces of wood tightly to your work surface so that you can use both your hands while you work with your tools.

The clamp's *frame* is C-shaped. Through one end of the frame runs a large metal *screw*. When you turn the *handle* on the screw, the screw moves closer to the other end of the frame. Whatever you put between the screw and the frame's end will be tightly gripped when you tighten the clamp.

You can either clamp your work piece flat on your work surface, or you can clamp it so that it stands straight up and down. Choose the position that will make your work easiest. Shifting boards can mean a ruined project, so no matter which position your C-clamp is in, always check to see that it's tightened securely. (Two C-clamps are even better than one, especially when you're working on longer boards.) Also make sure that the clamp doesn't get in the way of the tools you're using; cast iron is hard on saw teeth! Readjust your clamp and your work piece whenever necessary.

USING YOUR HAMMER

A hammer has two main parts: a large *head* and a long *handle*. You'll use the flattened, circular *face* on its head to pound nails and to tap one piece of wood so that it lines up with another before you nail the two pieces together. The steel *claw* is for pulling out nails that are bent or in the wrong place.

Hammering Nails

When they're struck by your hammer, nails can fly through the air instead of going into the wood. Flying nails can hurt your eyes, so protect yourself by putting on your *plastic safety goggles* whenever you plan to start hammering.

Before you hammer any nails into your projects, you'll want to get some practice by hammering common nails into scrap wood. Common nails have bigger heads than finishing nails and are easier to pound. Get a feel for how to hold your hammer and how to swing it the right way. Soon you'll be a pro! (To learn more about using nails, see "All About Nails" on pages 33–34.)

First, grip the hammer handle in your right hand (or in your left if you're a lefty). The further from the head you hold the handle, the more power you'll have, but grip the handle wherever it feels best to you. Turn the steel face down and away from you, and line up the handle with your elbow.

Next, with the index finger and thumb of your other hand, set the nail's point down where you want it to enter the wood, making sure to hold the nail straight up and down. Tilting the nail will make it bend or go out the side of the wood when you pound it.

To start the nail, tap its head several times with the hammer's face until the point of the nail sticks into the wood. Then move your hand from the nail, and use it to steady the board instead.

Keep your eyes on the nail's head as you swing the hammer down onto it, and hit the nail sharply. If the nail doesn't sink into the wood, you probably need to hit it harder. Swing your hammer from the elbow and arm so that you're using the power of your whole upper body, not just the power in your wrist. Swing carefully and steadily. As the nail sinks into the wood, try not to dent the wood with the hammer. With those last few swings, hit the nail lightly until the nail's head is flat on the wood's surface.

Pulling a Bent Nail or One That's Driven in Crooked

When you need to pull out a bent nail, grip it with the V-shaped hammer claw, and place the steel top of the hammer flat on the wood next to the nail, with the handle straight up and down. Use one hand or a helper to hold your wood flat on the work surface. With the other hand, pull the handle down towards the board and away from the nail until the nail pops out. If you're having a rough time, put a scrap of wood under the hammer's head before you pull back on the handle. You'll then find it easier to pull the nail out.

When the point of a nail comes out in the wrong place, and you can't pull the nail out because you can't reach its head, turn the board over, and hammer the pointed end of the nail back into the wood. Then turn the wood back over again, and use the claw to pull the nail out. Start a new nail in a different spot.

To learn more about joints (how boards fit together for nailing) see "All About Joints" on pages 34–35.

  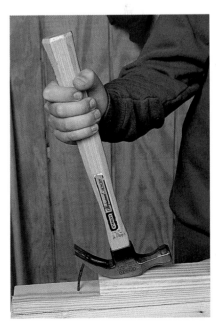

USING YOUR HANDSAW

The saw you'll need for these projects is a *crosscut handsaw*. This type of saw can cut straight lines both *across the grain* (across a board's face) and *along the grain* (in the same direction as the board's edge). Buy a saw with a wood *handle*, one that feels comfortable to you when you grip it. Avoid buying a ripsaw; it isn't designed to cut across the grain of a board.

The saw's metal *blade*, which is fastened to the handle with screws, is strong and flexible so that it won't bend and break when it's used correctly. On one edge of the blade is a row of sharp teeth; the blade's other edge (called the *back*) is flat. As they cut, the teeth sink down into the wood, making a groove called a *kerf*. Because the teeth (and the kerf that they make) are slightly wider than the blade's back, the saw doesn't stick as it cuts into the wood.

Never use a saw with teeth that are bent, broken, or dulled or a handle that is loosely attached to the blade. Nothing is more aggravating (or dangerous) than working with a beaten-up handsaw!

Keep your handsaw in good shape by storing it so that its teeth don't bump against other metal tools. Have an adult helper check the teeth occasionally to see that they're sharp. A local "sharp shop" can touch them up when they're dull.

Securing Your Work for Sawing

If you're right-handed, clamp your work piece to the work surface so that the line you plan to cut hangs over the right edge of the work surface by about 2". If you're a lefty, switch the work to the work surface's left edge.

Starting Your Saw-Cut

Using a handsaw isn't difficult, but have an adult helper give you a hand so that you get a good start with this important skill.

Keep in mind that as the saw's teeth cut, they remove about 1/16" of the wood that you're cutting. This can change the length of your work piece. If, for instance, you've measured and marked a line 8" from the squared end of a board, and you saw right on top of the line you've drawn, the piece you cut will be a little shorter than 8". When you start your saw-cut, don't put the blade right on the line you've measured and marked. Instead, place the teeth slightly to one side of the line, on the *waste* side (or side that you won't use). By keeping your saw blade off the wood you plan to use, your cut pieces will always be exactly as long as you measured them.

If you try to saw back and forth on a board right away, you may chip off part of the board, and your saw may also jump around. To begin a cut properly, set the saw blade down where the line you marked meets the edge of the board that's farthest away from you. Remember, the blade should be on the waste side of the line. Next, set the thumb of your free hand lightly against the saw blade's side, just above the teeth. Pull the saw lightly back towards you; it will make a little groove in the wood. Lift the saw up, move it away from you, and set it into the groove that you just cut. Then pull the saw back towards you again. Repeat this process several times until the groove deepens a bit. Now you're ready to begin sawing!

Body Power

Grip your saw's handle with one hand, and as you cut, line up your arm and shoulder behind the blade. This position puts the power of your upper body behind the saw and will make sawing easier. Place your other hand on your work piece (well away from the saw's teeth), plant both feet a little apart, and keep your body behind the saw and the board you're cutting.

Sawing Straight and True

Saw back and forth, tilting the point of the saw at an angle towards the ground. Cut slowly and steadily, taking breaks whenever you need them. Keep the blade square to the board; don't let it lean to the left or right. The blade should follow your marked line. If it begins to wander, guide it back by very lightly twisting the handle as you saw. Keep your eyes on the marked line, and you're sawing straight and true!

Common Sense Sawing

Never saw freehand; if you do, you won't like the results! Always mark and saw along a pencil line that's straight and square.

Have your helper support the wood that hangs over the edge of your work surface so that it doesn't tear off as you finish your saw-cut.

Now and then, when you're cutting a type of wood that you don't use often (such as a dowel or a piece of lattice), you'll have to make a saw-cut that doesn't quite match the instructions given above. Think about how the saw-cut can be made safely and accurately. Then fasten your work piece securely, and make your cut. Let common sense be your guide, and get a little advice from your adult helper too!

To learn about joints (how boards fit together), see "All About Joints" on pages 34–35.

USING YOUR TWIST DRILL

Also called a *hand drill*, this tool looks a little bit like an eggbeater. Instead of beaters, though, it has a *chuck* at one end—a small clamp that grips the *drill bit* used to bore the hole. At the other end of the drill is a *handle* to steady the tool, and in the middle is a *crank*, which is attached to a set of *gears*. When the crank is turned, the gears spin the chuck (and the bit in it) rapidly. A little pressure on the handle forces the bit into the wood.

The twist drill bores small holes into wood. (You'll use a brace and bit to bore larger holes.) Only two twist drill bits are necessary for these projects: 1/8" and 5/32".

Protect Your Work Surface

Before you clamp your work piece down, put a piece of old scrap wood between it and your work surface. This scrap will keep the drill bit from boring holes into your work surface!

Have Your Helper Steady the Work

Sometimes (with a right-angle joint, for instance) two pieces of wood can't be clamped securely. When you're boring a hole through pieces like this, have a helper hold them firmly in position while you bore the hole.

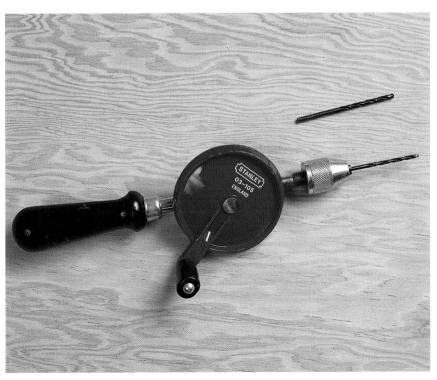

Dimple Your Work Before Boring

Unless you tell the drill bit's tip where to enter the wood's surface, it will slip around on top of the wood when you start to bore a hole. To avoid this problem, you can *dimple* the place where you plan to bore the hole. Set the sharp tip of a large nail right on the mark that you've made on the wood. Then make a small dimple in the wood by tapping the head of the nail once. This dimple will guide the drill bit as you bore into the wood. Be careful not to dimple (or bore) anywhere near a nail. The nail may break or dull the bit!

Choosing the Right Size and Type of Drill Bit

For the projects in this book, use either *twist drill bits* or *brad point bits.* A brad point bit has a sharp point, which centers the bit, and two, small sharp cutters on its ends. Brad point bits make boring holes easier, but they aren't available in all sizes, so use regular twist drill bits when you need to. They'll work just fine.

Using the right size bit is very important because each size makes a different size and kind of hole. The project instructions in this book will tell you which size bit is necessary. As you build some of these projects, you'll also learn about boring holes for different kinds of hardware and dowels.

Chucking a Drill Bit

Hold the drill in one hand. With your other hand, twist the chuck until it opens. If the chuck is stuck closed, you may need to hold the crank tightly with one hand while you turn the chuck firmly with the other. Slide the flat end of the drill bit all the way into the open chuck, and then turn the chuck in

Boring Pilot Holes for Screws

Driving a screw into wood is much easier when you've bored a *pilot hole* first. Boring a pilot hole removes most of the wood from the place where you plan to drive the screw. Just enough wood is left to grip the small threads of the screw tightly and guide it into the hole. A pilot hole must be exactly the right size for the required screw! To bore pilot holes for No. 8 screws, use a 1/8" drill bit; for larger No. 10 screws, use a 5/32" bit.

Flagging a Drill Bit

To bore a pilot hole to a certain depth, make a *flag*. First, find out how deep the screw hole needs to be. In this book, the project instructions will give you that depth. Then use your tape measure to measure exactly that distance up the drill bit, starting from its tip. (If you're using a brad point bit or a brace and bit instead of a twist drill bit, take your measurement from the bottom of the bit's cutters, not from its tip.) Wrap a piece of masking tape around the drill bit so that the bottom edge of the tape marks the distance you've measured (1-1/2" for a 1-1/2" screw, for instance). Then watch the masking tape flag as you bore, and stop boring the minute the flag touches the surface of the wood. It's a simple method, and it's accurate!

Other Drilling Tools

Ask someone at your local building supply store about countersink bits, drill-bit stops, and screw-sizing gauges. These helpful tools can make your work easier and your projects even better looking.

To learn more about using screws, read "Using Your Screwdriver" on the next page.

the opposite direction to tighten it around the bit.

Boring the Hole

After you've clamped and dimpled your work piece and have tightened the correct drill bit into the chuck, set the tip of the bit on the dimple you've made. Grip the drill's handle with one hand, and press down on it as you turn the crank quickly with your other hand. (Use your right hand to turn the crank if you're right-handed.) As the bit bores down into the wood, hold the twist drill straight up and down; don't let it lean to the left or right, back or

forth. Stop boring when the bit enters the scrap wood.

If you're boring a hole into a board that is clamped straight up and down instead of flat, hold the twist drill level to the ground, with the handle end against your chest. As you turn the crank, push forward into the wood.

To remove the bit from the finished hole, turn the crank in the opposite direction, and pull on the handle steadily until the drill bit pops out of the wood.

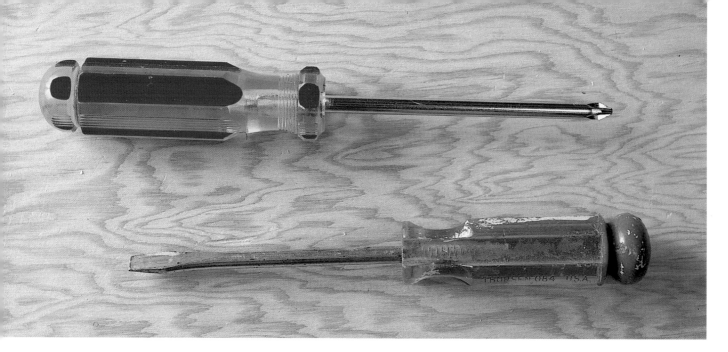

USING YOUR SCREWDRIVER

Screwdrivers are used to *drive* (or turn) screws into wood. They have three parts: a *handle*, a steel *shaft*, and a *tip*. The tip matters most because it's the working end of this tool. The tip of a *flat-bladed screwdriver* is used to drive slotted-head screws. The X-shaped tip of a *Phillips screwdriver* fits into the X on the head of a Phillips screw. Phillips screwdrivers have more driving power than flat-bladed screwdrivers, so use Phillips screws when you can find them in the right size for your project. But keep a flat-bladed screwdriver handy in case you can only find slotted-head screws!

Screwdriver tips come in different sizes as well as types. *No. 2* tips are medium-sized. They work well with the No. 8 and No. 10 size screws used for the projects in this book, so get a No. 2 Phillips screwdriver and a No. 2 flat-bladed screwdriver. As you build projects of your own design, you may need smaller or larger screws. For these, you'll want to add No. 1 and No. 3 screwdrivers of both types.

Driving a Screw

Before you pick up your screwdriver, always use your twist drill to bore a pilot hole the right size for the screw that you plan to use. To learn more about boring pilot holes, see "Using Your Twist Drill" on pages 25–27.

After you've bored the pilot hole, set the screwdriver's tip on the head of the screw, and then set the screw's point into the pilot hole.

Turn the screwdriver in a clockwise direction to drive the screw in; use the power in your shoulder as you do. Keep the screwdriver's tip centered in the head of the screw so that it won't slip out.

To learn more about screws, see "All About Screws" on page 34.

To learn more about joints (how boards fit together with screws), see "All About Joints" on pages 34–35.

USING YOUR COPING SAW

This strange-looking saw is used to cut curves (small circles, and longer flowing lines, for example). It has several parts: a C-shaped steel *frame*, two *pin holders* that grip the ends of a thin, sharp-toothed, *replaceable blade*, and an *adjustable handle* that loosens when you want to change blades. The pin holders rotate so that you can adjust the blade to cut in any direction. Because you can angle the blade this way, you'll be able to cut oddly shaped lines that no other saw can reach.

Unlike the handsaw, which cuts as you push it forward, this saw cuts wood as you pull the blade back; its teeth point back toward the handle. Two little pins, one at each end of the blade, are held tightly by the two pin holders on the frame's ends. This tension is what allows such a thin blade to cut through wood. If you loosen the handle so that the tension disappears, the blade flops around and won't cut correctly. Work with your adult helper until you get the hang of this tool!

Cutting Curves

First, you'll need to secure your work so that it doesn't move around while you cut it. If you can't remember how to do this, see "Using Your C-Clamp" on page 22.

Once your work is clamped, grip the saw's handle with one hand. Then set the blade on the edge of the wood, even with the line that you've marked, and begin pushing and pulling the saw back and forth. You don't have to "start" the cut as you do with the larger handsaw. Keep a little pressure on the blade, but don't bend or

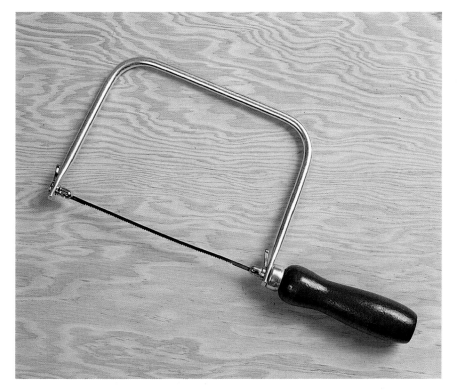

Tools & Techniques 29

break it by pressing too hard. Watch the marked line, and turn the handle slightly so that the blade follows that line. Don't turn the saw's blade too tightly to follow a curve, or the blade may bend or break. You'll get a feel for how tight your turns can be after you've used your saw for awhile. Keep the blade of your saw aimed in the direction you want to cut, and you won't go wrong.

To saw wood that's clamped flat to your work surface, you might be most comfortable kneeling on the ground and sawing up and down along the line.

If the saw's frame bangs against the outside of the wood (or against anything else), and you can't continue sawing along your marked line, turn both pin holders in the frame so that the frame is turned away from the obstacle, and then keep sawing. You might have to do this several times, depending on the size and shape of your work piece.

Making an Inside Cut

Sometimes you'll want to cut out a shape that is "inside" your work piece. (The square cutout in the bit bin project is a good example of this kind of shape.) Start by boring a hole at least 1/4" in size just inside of the shape that you want to cut out. Then remove the blade from your coping saw, slip the blade through the hole, and tighten the blade back into the saw frame. Now you can cut out the shape from the inside!

Replacing the Blade

This can be tricky. Four hands are better than two, so get some help!

If the blade isn't broken or missing, look closely at how the two pin holders grip it at each end. Then loosen the handle by turning it until you can remove the blade. Insert a new blade onto the two pin holders, turning the teeth back towards the handle. (You may need an extra hand to keep everything lined up.) Tighten the handle so that the blade is held tightly in the frame.

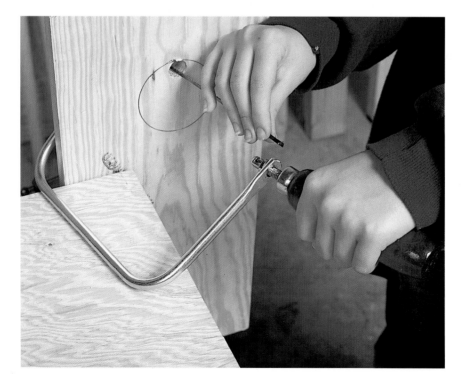

USING YOUR RASP

A rasp scrapes away a project's rough surfaces to make them smooth. It has two parts: a rounded *handle* and a long piece of *steel* that is covered with sharp teeth. The steel on a *half-round rasp* (the type of rasp that you need) has one flat side, to use on flat wood surfaces, and one curved side, for the inside of curved saw-cuts.

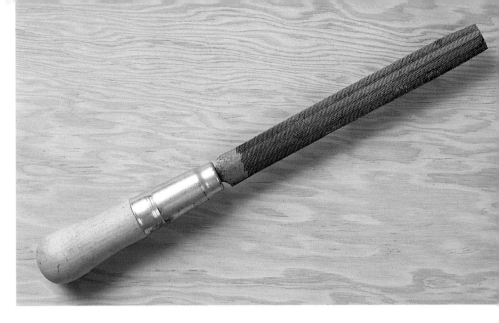

Clamp your work piece securely to your work surface. Hold the rasp's handle in one hand, and place the steel on your work piece. Now push the steel across the wood, keeping the rasp flat as you do. You may find it helpful to put a little pressure on the steel with the fingers of your other hand.

A rasp only smooths away wood as it's moving forward, so bring it back to the starting position by picking it up instead of pulling it back. Push forward again, lift up, and push forward, over and over, until you can't see or feel any rough surfaces on your work piece. Try to smooth out all the little lines left by the saw that you used. After you've rasped your work piece, you'll use sand-paper to finish smoothing it.

USING YOUR BRACE AND BIT

This tool bores larger holes than the twist drill can make. The *brace* (the curved part) has a round *handle* on its top, a second handle on its middle section, and a *chuck* at its bottom end. The bits (called *auger bits*) have three parts: a square or rounded *end* that fits into the brace's chuck, a spiral *shaft*, and a *screw-tipped end* with two *cutters* that do the actual boring. Bits comes in many sizes, but you'll only need five for the projects in this book: 1/4", 3/8", 1/2", 3/4", and 1". There's no way around the fact that this is an expensive tool, so try to find a used one (in good condition) for sale.

All Drills Have Some Things in Common

Like a twist drill, a brace and bit bores holes, but it's used a little differently. Because the screw-tip on the bit pulls the bit into the wood as you turn the brace, you don't have to press as hard on the rounded handle as you do on a twist drill's handle. You don't have to dimple the wood before you start, either, because the sharp screw-tip won't slide around when you begin boring; it will sink right into the wood.

Boring Holes with Your Brace and Bit

To learn all about chucking bits, securing your wood for boring, and other important tips, read "Using Your Twist Drill" on pages 25–27.

First, remember to sandwich a piece of scrap wood between the work piece and your work surface. Then set the bit's screw-tip on the marked and clamped wood. To start the bit into the wood, hold the brace's rounded

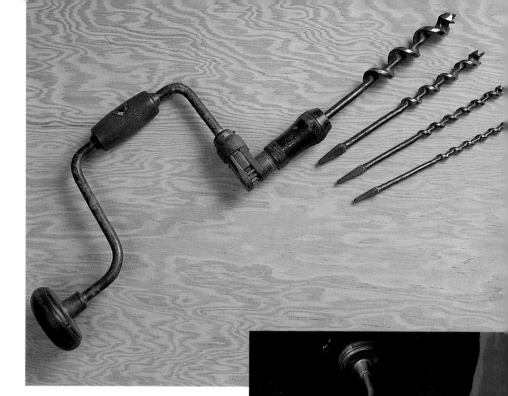

handle with one hand, and turn the crank handle with the other hand. Keep the brace and bit straight up and down so that the hole will be straight, too. (If your wood is clamped upright on your work surface, hold the brace and bit level with the ground instead.) Continue boring to finish the hole.

To remove the bit from the wood, ask your adult helper to give you a hand. Some braces have a switch or a collar that must be reversed to keep the chuck tight when you turn the brace backwards to pull out the bit.

Body Balance

You don't need much strength to use your brace and bit, but you do need good balance. You may find it easier to use this tool if you kneel on top of your work surface when you're boring wood that's clamped flat. This way, you'll be above the tool and will be able to control it better. You can also have a helper turn the crank while you concentrate on holding the brace and bit straight. If your

helper throws your balance off, each of you can put a hand on the top handle while one of you turns the crank.

Get a hand from your adult helper if you run into problems using this tool. Together, you'll figure it out!

For information on boring holes to a certain depth, see "Flagging a Drill Bit" on page 27.

ALL ABOUT GLUE

Wood glue *(carpenter's yellow glue)* and *white glue* are used to help hold pieces of wood together. Although it's strong, glue usually won't do a very good job without the help of extra fasteners: nails, screws, bolts, and other hardware.

The trick to successful gluing is in learning to apply just the right amount of glue—enough to make the pieces stick tightly together, but not so much that you end up with globs of glue dripping from your project! When you're gluing an end or an edge of one board to another board, run a thin line (about as wide as a 6d finishing nail) along the center of the end or edge. Then set the boards together, and drive nails or screws into them. When you're gluing the faces of two boards together, spread the glue lines around a bit, but don't make any lines thicker than a 6d finishing nail.

When glue drips or squeezes out from the project you're building, you've used too much. Wipe it up quickly with a damp paper towel. If the drips have already started to dry, you can peel them up like rubber. If they're really dry, ask an adult helper to give you a hand removing them before you sand and finish your project.

Glue takes awhile to dry, depending on the weather and how much glue you've used. It's best to be ready to nail or screw your boards together right after you put glue on them.

Epoxy resin glue is a super-strong glue that's sometimes used to glue two different materials together. It's sold in two parts that are mixed together before they're applied. Epoxy glue can be messy, so unless a project requires it, you should use regular yellow carpenter's glue or white glue instead.

No matter which glue you're using, keep dried glue peeled off the glue bottle's tip, and always put the cap back on as soon as you're finished squeezing out the glue.

ALL ABOUT NAILS

Nails are used, usually along with glue, to create the strong joints that hold projects together. Sold by the box or by the pound, they come in many types, sizes, and lengths. The three types you'll need for the projects in this book are *finishing nails*, *common nails*, and *brads*.

Finishing nails, which you'll use most often, are thin nails with very small heads—heads so small that you can barely see them once the nail has been driven into a piece of wood. These nearly invisible heads make them look a little neater on a project than common nails look. You'll use finishing nails when you fasten fairly thin pieces of lumber together (two 1 x 4s, for instance).

A common nail is thicker and stronger than a finishing nail. It has a wide head on one end and is used to nail together thicker pieces of wood, such as two 2 x 4s.

Brads look like tiny finishing nails. They're used to fasten thin pieces of wood, such as lattice strips, to one another.

Once you know what type of nail you want, you'll need to know the name for its size. Nail sizes are identified with the "d" symbol, which stands for penny. A 2-1/2" common nail, for example, is called an *8d* (or 8-penny) common nail. It's very important to use the right type and size of nail; just look at the Materials list for your project to find out which nails are required.

Keep a pound or so of the larger nails on hand. They don't cost much, and you can always use the extras on another project. A small box of brads is plenty. To keep your nails and other hardware organized, collect and recycle clean tin cans and small jars. Use a different container for each type of hardware, and store them all in a cardboard box near your workbench.

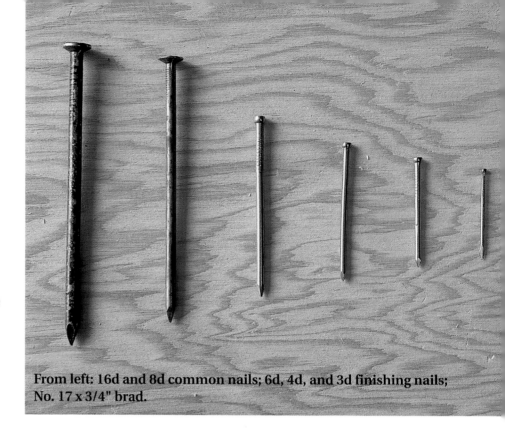

From left: 16d and 8d common nails; 6d, 4d, and 3d finishing nails; No. 17 x 3/4" brad.

ALL ABOUT SCREWS

A screw has three parts: a *head*, a *shank*, and *spiral threads* that end in a sharp point. A screw's job is to hold pieces of wood together, which it does by gripping the wood with its sharp metal threads. The twist in these threads is what pulls the screw into the wood as the head is turned by a screwdriver. In the old days, threads were cut by hand, one screw at a time. Today, machine-made screws are as common as nails.

Screws come in many types, and each type comes in different sizes and lengths. For these projects, you'll use only two types: *flathead Phillips screws* and *flathead slotted screws*. The first word in their names (flathead) describes how the tops of their heads fit against the wood: nice and flat! The sec-

ond word (Phillips or slotted) describes the tool that's used to drive the screw—either a Phillips screwdriver or a flat-bladed screwdriver. The slotted screw has just one straight slot on its head; the Phillips screw has two slots that cross to make an X shape. When you buy screws, get the Phillips type if they're available because they're easier to drive into the wood. Either type will get the job done, though.

Screws are sized by their thickness (No. 8, No. 10, etc.; the smaller the number, the smaller the screw), and by their length. For these projects, you'll only need a few different lengths of *No. 8* and *No. 10* screws. The Materials list that comes with your project will tell you which screws you'll need.

To learn more about using screws, see "Using Your Screwdriver" on page 28.

ALL ABOUT JOINTS

A joint is the place where two boards meet when they're fastened together. Strong joints will make your projects look their best and last a long time. The projects in this book make use of only two types of joints.

When one board is fastened to another board to make a right angle, it's called a *right-angle joint*. These joints are also called *butt joints* because one piece of wood butts up against another. One butt joint on its own isn't very strong; there isn't much wood where the two boards meet, so the boards can flop around. Several right-angle joints put together, however, make a really strong project. A box, for example, uses lots of right-angle joints to add strength. Have you heard of "strength in numbers"? Well, this is it!

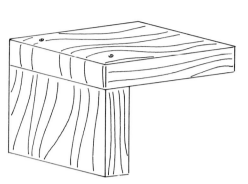

Right-angle (or butt) joint

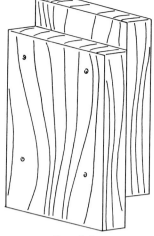

Face joint

When you fasten two boards together so that their faces are flat against each other, you're making a *face joint*. This joint is very strong by itself because so much wood is fastened together in one place.

Making Strong Joints
There are two keys to making a strong joint. First, make sure that the pieces you want to join are sawed squarely so that they'll fit together correctly. Second, put glue, nails, and screws in the right places. (The project instructions will tell you how to do this.)

To learn more about making strong joints, see "All About Glue" on page 33, "All About Nails" on pages 33–34, and "All about Screws" on page 34.

ALL ABOUT SANDING
Can you imagine holding a baseball bat with a handle that's rough and square instead of round and smooth? Or getting splinters when you pat a wooden doll's head? Sanding smooths out the roughness left by the tools that you used to build your project. It also gets the wood surface ready for finishing. Because sanding

creates a lot of floating sawdust, you should wear a paper dustmask to help keep the sawdust out of your lungs. Ask for these when you buy your sandpaper.

Sandpaper
There are many different kinds of sandpaper, but for this book's projects, you'll use just one, in two different sizes. Like all sandpaper, *garnet sandpaper* consists of a heavy paper backing covered with tiny fragments of crushed rock (in this case, garnet rock). The size of the rock fragments is

indicated on the package. You'll need both *100-grit* and *150-grit* garnet sandpaper. You can substitute another kind of sandpaper if you can't find garnet, but try to get both grit sizes.

100-grit sandpaper is used first because its larger pieces of garnet cut rough wood quickly. 150-grit paper gives an extra-smooth surface; you use it after you've taken off the worst of the rough spots with 100-grit paper.

How to Sand Your Project
Fold a piece of sandpaper once or twice, and then rub the gritty side across the rough wood. Whenever you can, rub *with the grain* (in the same direction as the lines in your project's wood grain). This gives a smoother surface than rubbing across the grain.

As you sand, wipe the sawdust off and check the edges, corners, and flat surfaces of your project to make sure that you're sanding them all carefully. Your goal is to get rid of all the sharp edges, but you don't want to sand so much that every edge is rounded. A good light will help you to spot

little saw marks and other problems that you might miss if your work area were dark.

To sand large flat surfaces quickly and evenly, wrap the sandpaper around a block of wood about the size of your hand. Then grip and push the block so that the sandpaper slides across your project.

Wipe the sawdust from your project, and check all its parts carefully, touching up any spots that still feel rough. Feels great, doesn't it?

ALL ABOUT TRACING PATTERNS

When you want to copy a pattern or drawing from a sheet of paper to a piece of wood, here's an easy way to do it.

First, make sure that you have a piece of *tracing paper* (from an art supply store), a piece of *carbon paper* (from an office supply store), and a *flat piece of wood*. Set the pattern sheet flat on your work surface, and put a piece of tracing paper on top of it. You'll see the pattern's shape through the tracing paper.

Next, trace the pattern onto the tracing paper. Press lightly with your pencil so that its point doesn't damage the paper. Then place your wood on the work surface, and put a piece of carbon paper (smudgy side down) on top of the wood. Place the tracing paper on top of the carbon paper, making sure that the shape you traced is on top of the wood and not hanging over any of its edges.

Now trace over the tracing. Press firmly so that the carbon paper will transfer the lines to the wood as you trace over them with your pencil. You're ready to cut out the shape with one of your saws!

ALL ABOUT FINISHING

Sand Before You Finish

Before you put a finish on your project, be sure to read "All About Sanding," which starts on page 35. Rough surfaces don't like paint, stain, or varnish, so careful sanding is an important part of finishing work.

Finish What You Started!

Projects meant for heavy use, such as the workbench, need only sanding, but most of the others will look their best and will last longer if you finish them. Some finishes protect wood; the hard coating formed by *paint* or *varnish*, for instance, will seal your project off from dirt and dampness. Other finishes, such as *stains*, just color the wood without sealing it, so a clear coat of varnish is usually applied on top of a stain.

Choosing a Finish

Each finish gives wood a different appearance. Before you buy a finish, decide what you want your project to look like. Then tell the salesperson where you buy your materials how big your project is and how you want it to look. Ask questions until you know what to buy and how to use it.

Latex Paints

Paint covers the good-looking grain of the wood completely, but it comes in many attractive colors. The paint that we recommend—*latex enamel*—is made with water, so after you've finished painting, you can clean up your paintbrushes (and any drips and spills) with warm water. The word *enamel* tells you that the paint is tough.

High-gloss latex enamel paint will make your projects shiny. If you don't want your project to gleam in the sunlight, use *semi-gloss* paint (sort of shiny) or *flat* paint (not shiny). If you plan to use your project outdoors, look for the word *exterior* on the paint can's label. If your project is going to stay indoors, choose an *interior* paint instead.

Oil-Based Stains and Varnishes

Stains add a little bit of color to wood, but they don't hide the wood's attractive grain. They don't protect the wood either, so after you've applied a stain, you'll want to brush on one or two coats of clear varnish. You'll find many different colors of stain from which to choose.

Varnish is a colorless, protective finish that lets the wood grain show through. It can be applied to wood whether the wood has been stained or not and gives all wood a nice glow. High-gloss varnish is very shiny; *satin* varnish isn't quite as shiny. (If it's available at your local paint store, you can get a combination stain-varnish instead of the two separate cans of finish. This product does both jobs; it colors the wood and protects it too.)

Don't let oil-based stain or varnish get on your clothing, your hands, or anywhere else it's not wanted!

Other Finishing Materials
In addition to paint, stain, or varnish, you'll need to add the following materials to your finishing kit: paintbrushes, mineral spirits or turpentine, newspapers and rags, stirring sticks, and old clothes to wear while you work.

Have you ever heard the saying, "Oil and water don't mix"? Well, they don't! Because most varnishes and stains are made with oil, if you try to use water to clean up after you apply them, you'll only make more of a mess! Instead, you need to rinse out your brushes and clean up your spills with *mineral spirits* or *turpentine*. (If you can find a water-based varnish, by all means use it!)

You can also use these two products to *thin* stains and varnishes. Think of toothpaste—it's thick, right? And milk is thin. Which one would soak into a tablecloth more quickly? Milk, of course. Thinned stains and varnishes soak into a wood's surface better than thick ones.

Buy the best *paintbrushes* that you can afford. Inexpensive ones

leave a trail of sticky hairs behind them! With the three sizes listed on page 12, you can complete every painting and staining job in this book.

Whenever you paint or stain a project, protect your work surface by covering it with lots of *newspapers*. Before you start painting, also make sure that you've got some clean *rags* and a bucket of water nearby (for cleaning up spills and wiping off hands). When you apply stain or varnish, you won't need the water; get out those mineral spirits or turpentine instead!

Thin pieces of scrap wood (dowels work well) make perfect *stirring sticks*. Just be sure that you've wiped all the sawdust off your stick before you use it. When you're through with it, put the stick straight into the trash; the drying paint, stain, or varnish on it will "glue" the wood to anything it rests on.

Putting on Your Finish
Many finishes give off dangerous and flammable fumes, so when the weather's good, finish your projects outdoors. If you have to work indoors, be sure that there's plenty of fresh air in your workshop, and stay far away from any sources of heat or open flame.

Before you grab your paintbrushes, wipe every speck of sawdust and dirt from your work surface, your project, and (if you're indoors) the floor. Dust that sticks to the finish will ruin its smooth surface. Then set out your finishing materials on your covered work surface. Next, read the instructions on the finish's label. They'll tell you exactly how to use the product safely and how to get the best results.

If you're using paint or varnish, open the can with a screwdriver, and stir the finish well with your clean stirring stick. Then brush it onto the wood *with the grain* (in the same direction as the long grain). Don't touch the finish with your fingers, and don't put too much on your brush, or it will drip. A light coat is all you want. Once it's on, let the finish dry well.

After the first coat of paint or varnish dries, sand it very lightly with 150-grit sandpaper—just enough to remove the bits of grain and sawdust that the finish lifts above the surface. Then wipe the project off carefully, and put on a second coat. At least two coats of paint or varnish should go on every project that you finish.

If you're using a stain, first stir it well. To see what your stain will look like before you apply it to your project, brush some on a scrap of the same wood as you used for the project. The more stain you put on, the darker the wood gets, so go easy until you're sure how much to use! If you like what you see, brush the stain onto your project or wipe it on with a rag. After the stain is dry, put on two coats of varnish. Your project looks great, doesn't it?

After You've Finished
Carefully rinse your paint-covered brushes in warm water. If you're using oil-based finishes instead of paint, place your brushes in a small bucket or large can, and clean them with mineral spirits or turpentine. Dry the brush tips with a clean rag, and pour the used spirits or turpentine back into the can. (You can re-use these products again and again.) Cap your cans and put everything away. Now you've really got the finishing touch!

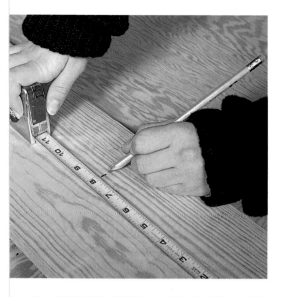

8. Take the clamp off, and hook the curved end of the tape measure over the end that you just squared.

9. Measure and mark a point 8" from the squared end.

10. Use your try square and a pencil to mark a line through the 8" point, across the board's face. Make this line square, too, by checking to see that the square's handle is flat against the board's edge before you draw your line. If the blade of the try square won't reach all the way across the 1 x 8, flip the handle to the other edge, line up the blade with the line you've already drawn, and finish the line with your pencil.

11. Secure the board with the clamp again, and cut along the line. Keep the 1 x 8 x 8" base that you've just cut, and put the scrap wood in your scrap bin.

12. Now use your marking tools, clamp, and handsaw to square one end of the 1 x 2 board. Then cut two strips from it; make each one 8" long. When you're finished, you'll have a total of three pieces. Store all the scraps in your scrap bin.

13. Put on a pair of safety glasses, and make sure that your helper does, too.

14. Next, have your helper set the base on its edge (not its end) on your work surface. Remember, the edge has the long grain.

15. While your friend holds the base, put a thin line of glue on its top edge—the one facing straight up.

16. Then put one of the strips flat on the base's gluey edge so that the strip's edge is even with the base's face. Have your friend hold

the base and strip together while you take the next step.

17. Hold your hammer firmly in one hand, and a 6d finishing nail in the other. Start the nail into the strip's face by tapping it lightly several times until its tip goes into the wood, about 3/8" from the strip's edge, near one end. Once you've started the nail, keep your eye right on its head as you hammer it through the strip and into the base. Keep your whole arm in line with the hammer (just as you did when you were sawing), and keep it fairly relaxed, too.

18. Now hammer two or three more nails into the strip, spacing them evenly, several inches apart. If a nail slants (and comes out one face of the base), turn the base upside down, and hammer the nail back out a little way. Turn the base over again, and use the hammer claw to pull the nail out. Hammer a new nail in, but don't use the same hole. You'll get the hang of it!

19. Next, have your friend turn the nailed pieces over so that the strip is on the bottom.

20. Now glue and nail the other strip to the base's other edge, but make sure that this strip gets nailed so that the three pieces look like the letter S.

21. When you're through, wipe off any extra glue that you see.

22. Then use some 100-grit sandpaper to smooth your bench hook all over. Watch out for splinters!

Using Your Miter Box

Your miter box will be a big help when you're cutting dowels and other small pieces of wood that are difficult to hold with your fingers. Clamp (or hold) the miter box on your work surface, and set the piece you want to cut inside the box. Then line up the place you want to cut with the slot that you cut in the miter box. Hold the piece firmly against the box's back side with one hand, making sure that your fingers aren't in front of the cutting line. With your other hand, slip the teeth of your handsaw down into the miter box's slot, and cut right through the work piece. The slot will guide your saw for you so that it makes a nice square cut; you can't go wrong!

Miter Box

Making square cuts on round dowels and small pieces of wood is no problem with a miter box.

MATERIALS

1   1 x 4, at least 40" long
8   No. 10 x 1-1/2" flathead wood screws
    4d finishing nails
    Wood glue
    Sandpaper, 100-grit
    Masking tape

TOOLS

Marking tools   Hammer
C-clamp   Twist drill and 5/32" bit
Handsaw   Screwdriver

CUT LIST

3   1 x 4 x 12"   Sides and bottom

PUTTING IT TOGETHER

1. Clamp the 1 x 4 onto your work surface so that about 14" hangs over the end that you use when you saw. Check the overhanging end to see if it's square. If it's not, go ahead and square the end first before moving on to the next step.

2. With your marking tools, measure and mark a square line across your board, 12" from the squared end.

3. Cut along the marked line with your handsaw. This piece will be the bottom of your miter box.

4. Using your clamp, marking tools, and handsaw, cut two more pieces of 1 x 4, each 12" long. These will be the miter box's sides.

5. Have your helper hold the bottom on one long edge while you run a line of glue along the top edge.

6. Set a side piece flat on the bottom's gluey edge so that the side's edge lines up with the bottom's face. The two pieces should look like the letter L when they're seen from the side. Have your helper steady the pieces for you.

7. Hammer a 4d finishing nail down through the side's face and into the bottom's edge; place this nail near either end of the side's face and about 3/8" in from its edge. Then hammer another 4d finishing nail near the other end, also 3/8" in from the long edge.

8. Turn the nailed pieces over so that the bottom piece's other edge faces up. Run a line of glue

along this edge, and then set the second side piece on it so that this side piece matches the one you've already nailed in place. Nail it just as you did in Steps 6 and 7.

9. Clamp the miter box flat on one side, on the front edge of your work surface, with its open part facing you. (It should look like a C when you see it from one end.)

10. Next, you need to mark the positions for the screws that will hold the sides of your miter box to its bottom. With your pencil, make four X marks on the side piece that's on top of the clamped

Building Five Basic Tools 43

assembly, spacing them equally and 3/8" in from the long edge that's farthest away from you. Measure carefully, and be sure not to mark any spots near a nail!

11. *Dimple* (make a small hole in) each X mark by lightly tapping a large nail into the X with your hammer. Don't drive the nail in too far! These dimples will guide your drill bit so that it doesn't slide around when you bore the holes.

12. Tighten a 5/32" bit into the chuck of your twist drill. You'll use the drill to bore pilot holes for the screws.

13. Wrap a small bit of masking tape around the bit, 1-1/2" from its pointed end. This tape is called a *flag*; it will send you a message telling you how deep to drill for the 1-1/2" screws that you'll be using.

14. Holding your twist drill firmly with one hand, and turning the crank with the other hand, bore a hole straight down through one of the X marks until the flag just touches the wood. Press down on the top handle as you turn the crank. When the flag touches the wood, your hole is 1-1/2" deep; stop drilling! (If the drill bit isn't boring a hole, try pressing down a

little harder with the hand that's holding the drill.) To remove the drill bit from the wood, pull the drill up as you continue to turn the handle.

15. Bore holes through the other three marks in the same way.

16. Turn the miter box over so that the other side is facing up. Clamp it, mark it, and bore another four holes, just as you did in Steps 14 and 15.

17. Set a No. 10 x 1-1/2" screw into one hole. Then use your screwdriver to drive the screw down until its head is just even with the wood's surface. (Keep pressing down on the screwdriver as you turn it.)

18. Use your screwdriver to drive the other seven screws.

19. Turn the miter box over onto its bottom; the open section will now face up. On either top edge, measure 6" from one end, and mark that point with your pencil.

20. Next, use your try square and a pencil to square across both top edges right at the mark you made; use the try square blade as a ruler to draw a line across these edges.

21. Now turn your try square so that you can mark a line up and down on the face nearest you, using the line you just drew as a guide.

22. Clamp the miter box in place, with its open section facing up, and use your handsaw to carefully cut straight through both sides of the miter box along the lines you drew. Hold the saw blade level with the bottom of the box. Cut until the teeth of the saw just touch the bottom; you don't want to cut the bottom at all. It's really important that this double cut be straight, so keep your eye on the lines as you saw!

23. Sand all of the miter box's edges well.

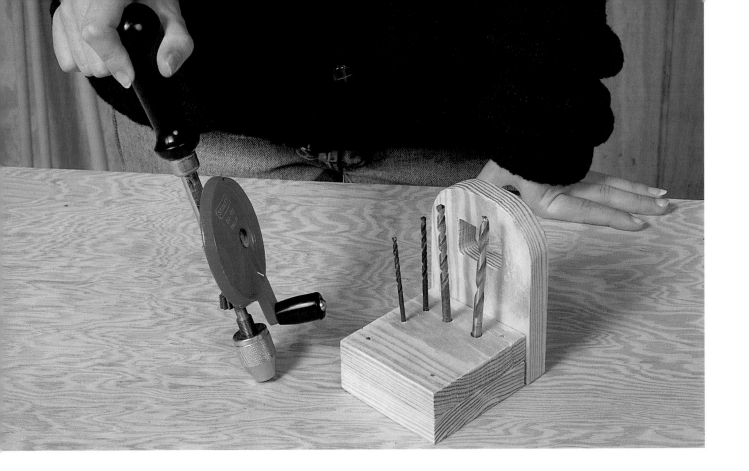

◆② **Bit Bin**

This easy-to-build container will keep your drill bits organized.

MATERIALS

1   Scrap 1 x 4, at least 20" long
    3d and 4d finishing nails
    Wood glue
    Sandpaper, 100-grit
    A jar lid, about 3" in diameter

TOOLS

Marking tools	Twist drill with all your bits
C-clamp	Coping saw
Handsaw	Brace with 1/4" bit
Hammer	Rasp

CUT LIST

1	1 x 4 x 5"	Back
2	1 x 4 x 3-1/2"	Base and bit holder

PUTTING IT TOGETHER

1. Clamp the scrap 1 x 4 flat onto your work surface, with at least 6" hanging over the edge that you use when you saw. With your marking tools, measure 5" from the overhanging end, and mark a square line. (Before you measure, remember to check the overhanging end to see that it's square! If it's not, square it before you measure and cut.)

2. Use your handsaw to cut along the marked 5" line. This piece will be the back of your bit bin.

3. Now use your clamp, marking tools, and handsaw to cut two 3-1/2" pieces of 1 x 4. These will be the bin's base and bit holder.

4. Rest the back flat on your work surface. Then, using the photographs as guides, draw the two curved lines and the inside shape for the cutout on the back's face, toward one end. A jar lid will help you to draw the curves. The cutout's size doesn't have to be exact; you'll use it to hang your bit bin on a nail. Make the cutout about 1" tall and 1-1/2" wide, and center it about 1-1/2" from the end with the curves.

5. Next, clamp the back upright onto the edge of your work surface. With your coping saw, cut along the two curves that you drew. Then, with your brace and a 1/4" bit, bore a hole just inside the cutout shape that you drew. Use a coping saw to cut the shape out. Start the cut by taking the

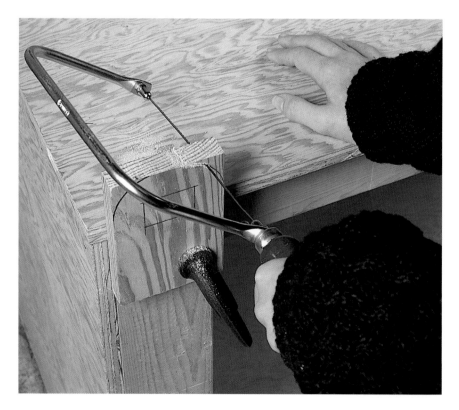

blade out of the frame, slipping it through the bored hole, and reattaching it to the frame. Grip the saw's handle firmly as you cut. You might find it easier to saw this way if you kneel. Keep your eye on the line, and make sure that the thin blade follows it as you saw. When you get to a spot where the line turns a corner, twist the handle to follow the direction of the line, but don't turn the handle too sharply, or the blade will break. You'll get the hang of it with a little practice!

6. When you're finished cutting, use your rasp to remove the rough edges from the inside of the cutout section and from the outside curves. Hold the rasp firmly, and keep it level with the edge you're working on. Push the rasp forward, rubbing it across the rough edge to scrape and smooth the wood. Keep rasping until the edge looks and feels smooth. Touch up the small inside curves with sandpaper.

7. Now clamp the bit holder flat onto your work surface, with a piece of scrap wood sandwiched between.

8. Count your twist drill bits. Mark an X (one for each bit) on the holder's top face wherever you want each bit to go. Keep these marks at least 3/4" apart from each other, and 3/4" away from the holder's edges.

9. Next, bore a hole right through each X mark and into the scrap, using your twist drill and a bit. The trick is to use a different bit to bore each hole; this way, every bit will bore its own new home to just the right size! (Be careful not to bore all the way through the scrap piece, or you'll damage your work surface.)

Building Five Basic Tools 47

10. Set the base flat on your work surface. Put a little glue on its top face.

11. Put the bit holder on top of the base, and line up all the edges just right.

12. Hammer a 3d finishing nail down into each corner so that each nail goes through both pieces.

13. Have a friend hold the glued pieces on edge, with the back edge facing up. Put a little glue on that edge.

14. Set the back's face flat on the gluey edge so that its square end (not the end with the cutout) is lined up with the base's bottom face.

15. Hammer several 4d nails through the back and into the base.

16. Sand your bit bin carefully, and wipe the sawdust off. (If you paint your bin, don't let any paint get into the holes.) Then store your bits away until you

start your next project! Label each hole with the bit size it holds, if you like. And when you add new

drill bits to your collection, keep them organized by boring a new hole for each one!

② Tool Box

Every builder needs a sturdy tool box!

MATERIALS

1   1 x 6 x 8'
1   1" dowel, at least 21" long
    4d and 6d finishing nails
    Wood glue
    Sandpaper, 100-grit

TOOLS

Marking tools   Hammer
C-clamp   Brace with 1" bit
Handsaw

CUT LIST

1   1 x 6 x 19-1/2"   Bottom
2   1 x 6 x 21"   Sides
2   1 x 6 x 11"   End panels
1   1" dowel, 21" long   Handle

PUTTING IT TOGETHER

1. First, make sure that the end of the 1 x 6 is square.

2. Then use your marking tools, clamp, and handsaw to cut a 19-1/2" bottom.

3. Repeat Steps 1 and 2 to cut two 21" sides and two 11" end panels.

4. Now you need to locate holes in the end panels for the toolbox's handle. First, use your tape measure and a pencil to measure and mark a line across one panel's face, 1-1/2" in from either end. Then measure and mark a short line at the same end, 2-3/4" from either long edge. Mark an X where the two lines meet.

5. Next, set a piece of scrap wood on your work surface. Place the two panels onto the scrap piece, lining up the marked panel on top of the other panel. Clamp all three pieces to your work surface.

6. Tighten a 1" bit into your brace, and using a little pressure, bore a hole through the X you just marked, right through the two end panels. Don't bore through the scrap piece! Pull the bit out often, and clean the wood chips from the bore hole to see if it's deep enough.

7. Run a line of glue along one end of the bottom piece. Have a helper hold it upright on the work surface or on the ground, with the gluey end at the top. Set the face of an end panel on the bottom's gluey end. Carefully line up the panel's end with the bottom's face, and make sure that the end of the panel with the hole in it is the end farthest away from the glue.

8. Hammer several 6d nails through the end panel, into the bottom.

9. Repeat Steps 7 and 8 to glue and nail the other end panel onto the other end of the bottom.

10. Set the nailed-up pieces on the work surface, with three edges lying flat. Measuring from the end of each panel that's attached to the bottom, measure and mark a point 5" along each panel's top edge.

11. Put a line of glue along the bottom piece's top edge. Also put a line of glue on each end panel's edge, but stop the glue line when you reach the 5" marks. You don't want to put glue all along these two edges!

12. Set a 21" side on the gluey edges so that one of its edges lines up with the bottom's outside face. Hammer 6d finishing nails through the side and into the bottom, spacing them several inches apart. Also drive a couple of nails through the side and into each end panel.

13. Turn the toolbox over, and repeat Steps 10-12 to attach the other side.

14. Now measure, mark, and cut a 21" piece of 1" dowel to make the handle. (Your bench hook or miter box will come in handy here!)

15. Slide the dowel through one hole in an end panel and on through the hole in the other panel so that the dowel ends line up with the panels' outside faces.

16. Set the toolbox on its bottom. Drive a 4d finishing nail down through the center of one end panel's top edge; the nail should go right into the 1" dowel. Drive another nail through the other end panel's edge. (These nails will keep the dowel handle secure.)

17. Sand your toolbox carefully to get rid of those sharp edges. Then load it up!

Workbench

A good workbench is the heart of any workshop. Here's a really rugged one that you can build in a weekend.

MATERIALS

1	2 x 4 x 10'
3	2 x 4 x 8'
1	4' x 8' x 5/8"-thick plywood
8	3/8" x 3-1/2" plated carriage bolts
8	3/8" washers

8	3/8" wing nuts
	16d common nails
	4d finishing nails
	Wood glue
	Sandpaper, 100-grit

TOOLS

Marking tools	Hammer
C-clamp	Brace with 3/8" bit
Handsaw	

CUT LIST

4	2 x 4 x 29-1/4" (cut from the 2 x 4 x 10')	Legs
4	2 x 4 x 21" (cut from one 2 x 4 x 8')	Leg braces
4	2 x 4 x 43-5/8" (cut from two 2 x 4 x 8' pieces)	Long braces
1	5/8" x 2' x 4' plywood	Work surface
1	5/8" x 2' x 4' plywood	Shelf
2	5/8" x 2' x 2' plywood	Sides

HINTS!

Have someone at the lumberyard cut your plywood for you.

As you build this work bench, take a look at the illustration. This type of drawing is called an *exploded view*. The artist "explodes" the bench so that you can see how every piece fits together. You'll find that the drawing will make your building job much easier.

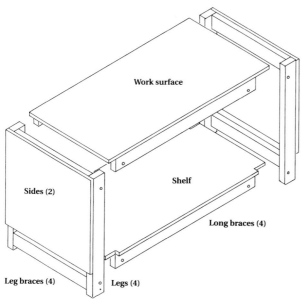

Work surface

Shelf

Sides (2)

Long braces (4)

Leg braces (4)   Legs (4)

PUTTING IT TOGETHER

1. Use your marking tools, clamp, and handsaw to cut the twelve pieces of 2 x 4 to the exact lengths in the Cut List. With your pencil, label each piece (leg, leg brace, or long brace) so that the boards won't get mixed up.

2. Set one 21" leg brace on the floor, with one end face up. Have a helper set the face of a 29-1/4" leg down on the leg brace's end. Line up one of the leg's edges with one face of the brace. Then hammer two 16d common nails through the leg and into the brace. (You might find it helpful to prop up the other end of the leg with another brace, just as the boys in the photograph are doing.)

3. Next, turn the nailed assembly over and nail the other leg to the brace so that it matches the first leg.

4. Have your helper stand the assembly on the floor, with the brace at the top. Then measure 1-1/8" from the bottom of each leg, and make marks on the inside faces of both legs.

5. Fit another 21" leg brace between the legs so that its bottom edge is even with the 1-1/8" marks you made. The brace's face should line up with the same edges of the legs as the other brace's face.

6. Turn the assembly onto its side so that you can drive two more 16d common nails through the leg and into one end of the brace. Flip the assembly over, and nail the other end of the brace in the same way.

7. Now repeat Steps 2-6 to make another leg-and-brace assembly with the other two legs and two 21" braces.

8. Rest one leg assembly on your work surface so that the legs' long edges rest on the work surface and the leg braces don't touch the surface at all. Measuring from the end of one leg that is even with its brace, measure 2' along the top edge of the leg, and make a mark. Measure and mark the other leg in the same way.

9. Put a line of glue along the top edge of each leg, running the line from the end that's even with the brace, all the way down to the 2' mark. Then put a third line of glue along the top face of the brace that is even with the legs' ends.

10. Set a 2' x 2' plywood side onto the assembly so that its top corners line up with the top ends of

the legs. If they won't line up, your assembly is not quite square; have an adult help you square the assembly before you continue. Then hammer 4d finishing nails through the side, into both legs and into the top brace. Space the nails about 4" apart.

11. Now repeat Steps 8, 9, and 10 to glue and nail the other plywood side onto the other leg assembly. Your leg assemblies are finished!

12. Set the 2' x 4' plywood shelf flat on your work surface. You're going to mark cutouts on this shelf so that it will fit around the legs. Measure the bottom end of a leg (it should be about 1-1/2" x 3-1/2"). Using your square and a pencil, draw a shape exactly that size on each corner of the piece of plywood. You can also do this by having a helper hold the end of a scrap 2 x 4 on the plywood's corner; then trace a rectangle around

the scrap's end onto the plywood. (The wide face of the shape you trace should line up with the shelf's long edge.)

13. While your helper holds the shelf steady, use your handsaw to cut out the four corners along the lines you drew.

14. Set two 43-5/8" long braces on the floor so that they sit on edge and are exactly 18" apart.

15. Put a line of glue along the top edge of each long brace.

16. Set the 2' x 4' shelf down onto the gluey long braces. The inside corner of each cutout should just line up with the outside face of each long brace. Use your tape measure at each of the shelf's corners to make sure that each short edge of the plywood is exactly 2-1/8" from the ends of the long braces. Also check both long sides of the shelf assembly to see that the plywood's long edge extends 1-1/2" beyond the brace's face.

17. When you've centered the shelf on the braces, hammer 4d finishing nails (one every 4") through the plywood and into the long braces. You've just finished the shelf!

18. To build the top of your workbench, you'll make an assembly just like the shelf assembly, but without the corner cutouts. Start by laying out and gluing the other two long braces and piece of plywood, just as you did in Steps 15 and 16.

19. After you've checked the measurements along the sides and at the corners, hammer 4d finishing nails through the plywood work surface and into the braces, just as you did in Step 17.

20. Before you can fasten the hardware to your bench, you'll need to set it up. Start by getting together a few helpers. Have one of them hold up a leg assembly, with its feet flat on the ground. Have another helper hold up the other leg assembly so that it's about 4' away from the first assembly. This distance doesn't have to be exact.

21. Now slide one end of the shelf into the bottom slot of a leg assembly, and then slide the other slotted leg assembly onto the shelf's other end. The shelf's braces should face the ground.

22. Next, get some help dropping the work surface assembly down onto the legs so that it fits just inside them. If you have trouble fitting the workbench pieces together, get an adult helper to give you a hand. Have your helpers hold the assembly together while you take the next steps.

23. Before you bore holes for hardware, you'll need to mark each leg. Measure and mark (near the top of one leg and on its outside face) 3" in from the outside edge of the plywood side. Then measure 3" down from the top of the work surface, and mark an X where the two measurements meet. Mark the other three top corners in the same way.

24. Mark the four bottoms of the legs, measuring in from each leg's outside edge and up from its end. This time, make both measurements 2-1/2".

25. While your helpers hold each corner of the bench tightly

Foozles and Flummadiddles

Foozle is an old word that means a mistake, a flub, or a foul-up. A *foozler* (the person who foozles) fluffs, goofs, and bungles, too. *Flummadiddle* is a slang word for anything you're working on, like your latest project. Flumadiddles can be doohickeys and thingumadoodles, too, depending on the number of gizmos, widgets, and do-funnies you stick on them. It gets pretty complicated!

If you find that you've foozled—made a crooked cut with your saw or hammered a nail the wrong way—you're in good company! Every woodworker foozles now and then; it's part of the challenge of learning to work with wood. Most flumadiddles have a foozle or two here and there, though you might not notice them.

In fact, even expert woodworkers can be foozlers. Builders sometimes make kitchen cabinets so big that they won't fit through the front doors of houses. And once in a great while, a whole crew of foozlers will put new wood siding or a brand-new porch onto the wrong house because they went to the wrong address. It really happens!

Keep in mind as you work that most mistakes can be corrected. Nails can be pulled; another board can be cut straight and true. No one likes to waste materi-

als or make mistakes, but we're all learning how to build, so if you foozle, don't feel frazzled! First fix your foozle, and then finish your flumadiddle.

together, use your brace and a 3/8" bit to bore a hole right through the legs and braces at each mark. You should have eight holes.

26. With your hammer, tap a 3/8" x 3-1/2" carriage bolt through a hole until the head sits flat against the leg. Then turn a washer and wing nut tightly onto the bolt's other end. Repeat for each hole that you bored. Your workbench will always be steady if you keep these wing nuts tight.

27. Carefully sand all the edges, and your workbench is ready to use! If you'll be taking your bench apart now and then for storage, use a pencil to mark the front side of the top shelf and legs. This will make it a lot easier to bolt your workbench back together again.

Part Four:
Pick Your Projects!

Watch Your Step!

To use your balance beam, set it on the floor or on the ground. See if you can walk the length of the beam without falling off. Try walking backwards on the beam or hopping along on one foot. Find out who can balance on one foot the longest. For a real test, try to balance on your hands! First sit with your hands placed together on the beam between your outstretched legs. Then straighten your arms, and lift yourself up a bit while you keep your legs straight out in front of you. What else can you do?

JUST FOR FUN

 Balance Beam

Can you walk the plank?

MATERIALS

1   2 x 6 x 10'
     Sandpaper, 100-grit
     A jar lid, about 4" in diameter

TOOLS

Marking tools   Coping saw
C-clamp   Rasp
Handsaw

CUT LIST

1   2 x 6 x 7'   Beam
2   2 x 6 x 18"   Legs

PUTTING IT TOGETHER

1. Have a friend help you set the 2 x 6 so that about 20" hangs over the edge of your work surface. Clamp the end nearest the 20" overhang.

2. Use your marking tools to mark a line 18" from the overhanging end.

3. Cut the squared line with your handsaw.

4. Repeat Steps 1-3 to mark and cut another 18" leg from the 2 x 6.

5. Using your pencil and tape measure, make a mark on one face of the 7' beam that remains; this mark should be exactly 3" from one end. Then make another mark, 4-9/16" from the same end.

6. Square two lines across the board, one through each mark.

7. Next, on each squared line, measure and mark 3" up from the beam's bottom edge. Then, using a scrap of wood as a ruler, draw a line with your pencil to connect these two 3" marks. As you can see, you've marked a notch; now you'll need to cut the notch out.

8. Have a friend hold the beam firmly on its edge, with the marked notch at the top. Use your handsaw to cut down the two lines to the 3" marks.

9. Then slip the blade of your coping saw down into one saw-cut, and cut across the line that connects the two saw-cuts. Remember to loosen the coping saw handle and turn the blade first so that it will cut along the line properly.

10. Repeat Steps 5-9 on the other end of the beam, making sure that this cutout is on the same edge of the board as the first one you made.

11. Now repeat Steps 5-9 on a leg, but make just one cutout in the center of one edge of the leg. You can do this by measuring across 8-1/4" and 9-13/16" before squaring and sawing. (All the cutouts in this project are the same size; only their locations change.)

12. Repeat Step 11 with the other leg.

13. To curve the top corners of the beam and legs, first set your jar lid on one face of the beam, in either of the corners that's on the edge opposite to the cutouts.

14. Use your pencil to draw a quarter-circle around the jar top; the line should touch the corner's edges.

15. While a friend holds the beam firmly, use your coping saw to cut the curved line that you just drew.

16. Repeat Steps 13-15 on the other end of the beam.

17. Repeat Steps 13-15 on each end of both legs, but make the curved lines and cuts on the same edge that the cutouts are on.

18. Sand all the pieces carefully, and wipe them off.

19. To put your balance beam together, set the legs on edge, either on the floor or outside on the ground. Make sure that their cutouts are facing up. Now set the beam down onto the two legs; its cutouts will fit into the legs' cutouts. If a joint doesn't quite fit, use your rasp in the tight cutout to remove a little wood. The cutouts should fit snugly, so be careful not to remove too much wood.

 **Rope Ladder**

How high can you climb? You decide!

MATERIALS

1   1 x 4 x 12'
    Sandpaper, 100-grit and 150-grit
    Masking tape
    1/2" braided nylon rope, 30' long
    Exterior latex enamel paint, any colors
    A stick for stirring
    1" paintbrush
    Rags and newspapers

TOOLS

Marking tools   Handsaw
C-clamp   Brace with 1/2" bit

CUT LIST

9   1 x 4 x 16"   Steps
2   Pieces of rope, each 15' long   Ladder sides

PUTTING IT TOGETHER

1. Set the 1 x 4 on its face on your work surface, and clamp it down. Use your marking tools and handsaw to cut nine steps, each 16" long.

2. On one of the steps that you've just cut, measure in 2" from each end, and make a pencil mark at each spot.

3. At each mark, use your try square and a pencil to mark a line across the step.

4. Measuring from an edge, mark the center of each line with an X. The center is at 1-3/4".

5. Now repeat Steps 2-4 with the other eight steps.

6. Clamp a step to your work surface, with a scrap piece sandwiched between them.

7. With your brace and 1/2" bit, bore holes right through the Xs on the step.

8. Repeat Steps 6 and 7 to bore holes in the other eight steps.

9. Sand all the steps carefully, including the holes you just bored. Use 100-grit sandpaper first; then use 150-grit for a really smooth surface.

10. Next, lay out the two pieces of rope on a flat surface. Starting 2" from the end of each rope, measure and mark off every 12" on both ropes.

11. Now tie a big knot at the 2" mark on each piece of rope. Make sure that the knot is bigger than the holes in the steps!

12. Slip a step onto both ropes so that it rests on the two knots. (The knots are below the steps, at the bottom of the rope ladder.) If you wrap some masking tape around the ropes' ends, you'll find it easier to slip them through the holes.

13. Then tie a knot at the first 12" mark that's above the step.

14. Slip another step onto the ropes, and slide it down until it rests on these new knots.

15. Continue tying knots at the 12" marks and sliding on steps until all nine steps are on the rope. You might need to adjust some of the knots to space the steps evenly.

16. Now measure and mark 14" up each rope from the last step, and knot both ropes together at the marks. Make this knot especially big and tight.

17. Paint the steps of your rope ladder any way you like; to make a rainbow rope ladder, paint each step a different color!

18. Get someone to help you hang your rope ladder from a sturdy tree branch (one that's at least 5" thick) or from any other climbing support that's 9' or 10' above soft ground. Always tie your rope ladder tightly to your climbing support. Use several knots, and make sure the support is strong enough to hold your weight. Now go to it!

 **Adjustable Stilts**

How's the weather up there, Longlegs?

MATERIALS

1   Scrap 2 x 4, at least 16" long
2   Scrap 2 x 2s, at least 55" long
1   Scrap 1 x 2, at least 16" long
4   Hex or carriage bolts, 3/8" x 6-1/2" or 7"
4   3/8" washers
4   3/8" wing nuts
    6d finishing nails
    Wood glue
    Sandpaper, 100-grit

TOOLS

Marking tools   Hammer
C-clamp   Brace with 3/8" bit
Handsaw

CUT LIST

2   2 x 4 x 6"   Steps
2   2 x 2 x 55"   Legs
2   1 x 2 x 6-3/4"   Braces

HINTS!

Study the *exploded view* illustration. Notice how the artist
has "exploded" the stilts so that you can see how every
piece fits together.

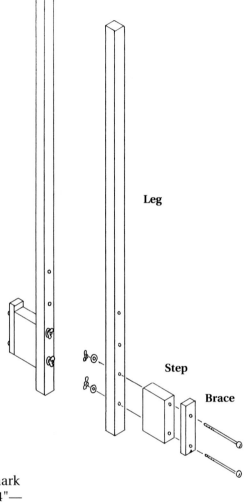

Leg

Step

Brace

PUTTING IT TOGETHER

1. Use your marking tools to square one 2 x 2 at 55".

2. Secure this piece to your work surface with your clamp, or have a friend hold one end firmly. Then cut along the pencil line with your handsaw. Repeat these steps with the other 2 x 2 to make another 55" leg.

3. Clamp one leg, with a piece of scrap wood under it, to your work surface. Place your tape measure at one end of the leg, and stretch it toward the other end. Starting

4" from the end of the leg, mark an X with your pencil every 4"— right down the exact center of the leg—until you have four marks. (The leg's center is at 3/4".)

4. Now use your brace and a 3/8" bit to bore four holes through the pencil marks. Be sure the scrap wood is under the marks you're boring.

5. Repeat Steps 3 and 4 with the other leg.

6. Next, secure the 2 x 4 to your work surface with a clamp. Let at least 8" of the board hang over the edge.

7. Measure, mark, and square the board, 6" from the overhanging end. Then clamp it and cut along the pencil line with your handsaw to make a step.

8. Repeat Step 7 to cut another 6" step from the leftover piece of 2 x 4.

9. Measure, mark, and square a 1 x 2 piece so that it's 6-3/4" long. Then clamp it and cut it with your handsaw. This will be a brace. Repeat this step to cut another brace from the leftover 1 x 2.

10. Set a step on your work surface so that it rests on its edge. Put some glue on the edge that faces up.

11. Put the flat face of one of the braces on top of the glue-covered step edge, so that 3/4" of the brace hangs over the end of the step. Then hammer a couple of 6d finishing nails through the brace and into the step piece. Place these nails close to the ends of the braces; you don't want them to interfere with the holes you'll be marking and boring in Steps 13, 14, and 15.

12. Repeat Steps 10 and 11 with the other step and brace.

13. Turn one of the assemblies over so that the brace is on the bottom and one edge of the step faces up. Starting at the end of the step that is even with the brace, measure and make two marks on the step's edge, at 1" and at 5".

14. Square across the step's edge at each mark. Then use your pencil to make an X at the center of each line. (The center is at 3/4".)

15. Now clamp one assembly to your work surface, with the marked edge of the step facing up. (Don't forget to put a piece of scrap wood under the step assembly!) With your brace and a 3/8" bit, bore a hole all the way through both X marks. Hold the brace and bit very straight, or your hole may come out the side of the assembly. Repeat to drill holes through the other assembly.

16. Sand all of your pieces really well, especially their sharp edges and corners.

17. To assemble your stilts, first find the two holes in one leg that are closest to the leg's end. Line up

Stepping Up in the World!

Use your stilts on soft ground, where the bottom ends won't slip and cause a fall. First make sure that you're holding them so that the step pieces face each other. Next, get a friend or two to help hold you steady while you put your feet on the step pieces. Once you're on, hold the leg pieces while you walk. (You may find balancing easier if you place the stilts' top ends behind your shoulders.) Stilts take a little getting used to! If you're feeling brave, raise the step pieces by assembling them in higher holes on the legs.

the two holes in an assembled step with the two holes near the end of the leg. Make sure that the step assembly isn't upside down! Now push 3/8" bolts all the way through the holes in the step until they come out through the holes in the leg. Put washers on the parts that stick out through the holes in the leg, and then tighten wing nuts on the washers. Repeat these steps to assemble the other stilt.

◈ Tic-Tac-Toe Game

Everyone who builds this game is a winner!

MATERIALS

1   Scrap 1 x 8, at least 20" long
1   Scrap 1/4" plywood, at least 7-1/4" x 12"
1   Scrap 1" dowel, at least 16" long
    3d finishing nails
    No. 17 x 3/4" brads
    Wood glue
    Sandpaper, 100-grit and 150-grit
    Latex enamel paint, four different colors
    A stick for stirring
    1" and 1/2" paintbrushes
    Rags and newspapers

HINTS!

If you don't have any 1/4" plywood handy, don't buy a whole new sheet for this small project. Instead, use any plywood scrap you have, no matter how thick it is. You can also use a piece of 1 x 8 that's the same size as the peg board. Your Tic-Tac-Toe Game will just be a little thicker.

If you don't have enough scrap 1 x 8, pick up a short board at your lumberyard.

TOOLS

Marking tools	Hammer
C-clamp	Brace with 1" bit
Handsaw	Rasp

CUT LIST

1	1 x 8 x 7-1/4"	Game board
1	1 x 8 x 12"	Peg board
1	1/4" x 7-1/4" x 12" plywood	Base
10	1" dowel pieces, 1-1/2" long	Pegs

PUTTING IT TOGETHER

1. This game is shaped like a sandwich. The square game board sits on top, the longer peg board lies in the middle, and the base rests below. Begin by using your marking tools, clamp, and handsaw to cut the game board and peg board.

2. Now use the same tools to measure, mark, and cut the plywood base.

3. Using the illustration as a guide, measure and mark the game board for boring and sawing. Draw the four lines first. Then mark nine Xs (for holes), one in the center of each square. To find the centers, just draw two diagonal lines in each square, from one corner to the opposite corner. These lines will cross at the centers.

4. Clamp the square game board, with a piece of scrap under it, face up on your work surface. Use your brace and a 1" bit to bore nine holes right through the nine marks that you've made. (Be careful not to bore through the scrap wood and into your work surface.) Remove the bit often to check on your progress.

5. You might need a hand here from an adult helper! Brush the wood chips off the top of the game board, and rest the teeth of your handsaw lightly along one of the four lines. Pull the saw back and forth a few times, keeping the teeth flat against the board and following the line. Don't tip the saw as you usually do for cutting; it should barely mark the lines on the game board's surface. Repeat this step to mark the other three lines with your saw.

6. Now, using the illustration as a guide again, mark the peg board for boring. You'll be marking for ten holes this time.

7. Clamp the peg board, with a piece of scrap under it, to your work surface. With your brace and a 1" bit, bore right through the ten marks that you've made.

8. With your marking tools and handsaw, cut ten 1" x 1-1/2" dowel pegs. (A miter box is the best tool to help you cut dowels.)

9. Test-fit a dowel peg in one of the game board's holes. The peg should fit loosely. If it's tight, hold it between your thumb and first finger while you use a rasp (held in your other hand) to remove some wood from the rounded side of the peg. Try to remove the wood evenly, turning the peg a bit as you go. Rasp all ten pegs to fit loosely in the holes.

10. Carefully sand the pegs and the three other parts with 100-grit (and then 150-grit) sandpaper, smoothing all the rough edges. Be sure the peg holes and peg ends are smooth, too. Wipe off the sawdust.

11. To assemble your Tic-Tac-Toe Game, set the game board on the work surface with its saw-marked lines facing down. Run a thin line of glue around the top face, about 1/4" in from the board's four outside edges.

12. Set the peg board down on top of the game board, with its holes facing down. Center the two boards carefully. The game board's two outside edges should line up exactly with the peg board's long edges, and the peg board should extend 2-3/8" over each end of the game board. Check these measurements with your tape measure, and adjust the pieces if necessary.

13. With your hammer, drive four 3d finishing nails through the peg board's face and into the game board, placing one nail at each corner.

14. Now run a few lines of glue here and there on the top of the peg board, which should still be face down on your work surface. Set the base on the gluey surface so that the edges line up all the way around. Then drive a few brads about 1/4" away from each edge to secure all three parts of the game together. (If you've used thick plywood or 1 x 8 material, you may need to use 3d finishing nails instead of brads.)

15. Sand any rough edges with 150-grit sandpaper, and wipe the sawdust off.

16. Using the photograph as a guide, apply two coats of paint to different parts of your Tic-Tac-Toe Game. Let each coat dry before you apply a second coat or another color. If you don't, the different colors may run together!

17. To play your new game, first find a friend. Choose your pegs, and then take turns putting one of your pegs into a hole. The object of the game is to be the first player to make a straight line with three of your pegs! The lines can run in any direction as long as they're straight.

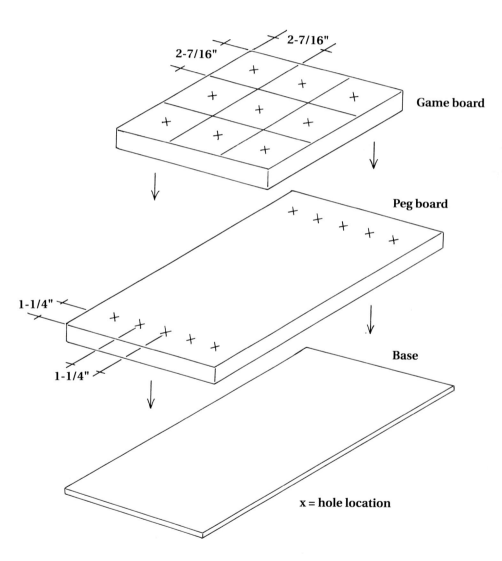

2-7/16"
2-7/16"
Game board
Peg board
1-1/4"
1-1/4"
Base
x = hole location

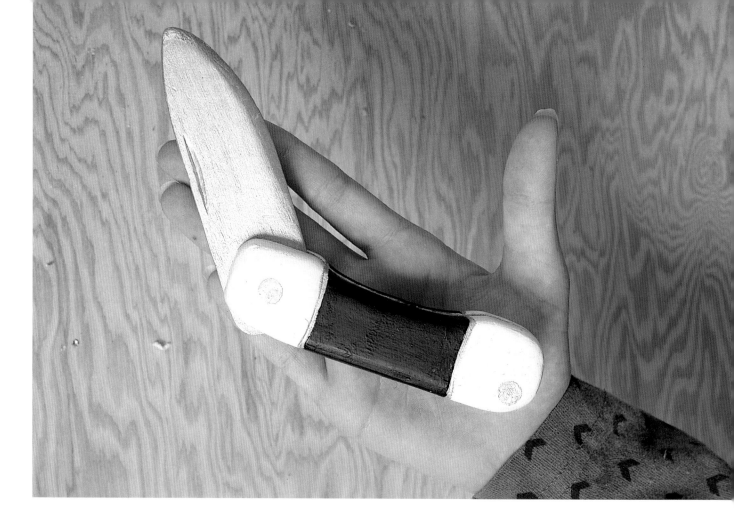

◆③ Pocket Knife

This dandy knife looks just like the real thing and is great fun to make.

MATERIALS

1   Scrap 1/4" x 1-1/2" lattice, at least 16" long
1   Scrap 1/4" dowel, at least 2" long
    Wood glue
    Sandpaper, 100-grit and 150-grit
    A sheet of tracing paper
    A sheet of carbon paper
    Latex enamel paint: white, black, and silver
    1/2" and detail paintbrushes
    A stick for stirring
    Rags and newspapers

TOOLS

Marking tools   Coping saw
C-clamp   Brace with 1/4" bit
Hammer   Rasp

PUTTING IT TOGETHER

1. Your knife has two parts: a case (made of two shaped pieces of wood held together by two dowels) and a flat blade (held in the case by one of those dowels). You'll begin by making the case. Have an adult helper give you a hand if you need one.

2. Set the scrap lattice flat on your work surface. Then take a look at the *full-scale* (or life-size) illustration of the knife. Transfer the pattern in the illustration to your lattice by following the instructions in "All About Tracing Patterns" (see page 36). To make two case pieces, you'll need to transfer the pattern at the bottom of the illustration twice. Be sure to trace the two marks on one case piece, too.

3. Clamp the lattice onto your work surface. With your coping saw, carefully cut out the two case pieces and the blade. Go easy with the saw; lattice is thinner than some other types of wood and may crack as you cut it.

4. Now match the two case pieces together, and clamp them to your work surface. Lightly smooth the rough edges with your rasp, until the two pieces match exactly. As you work, turn the pieces and re-clamp them as necessary.

5. Next, clamp the blade securely, and rasp all its edges smooth. Then remove the clamp. Holding the blade firmly in one hand, rasp along its curved edge (on both sides) to create a "sharp" edge. Don't try to make the edge too sharp, or it will break!

6. Be really careful with this step! Using the illustration as a guide, sandwich the blade between the two case pieces. Make sure that the case piece with the two marks on it is on top. Then place the stack on your work surface, with a piece of scrap wood under the stack. The case pieces' flat edges should face the edge of the work surface that's closest to you. The sharpened blade edge should also be facing you, and the pointed end of the blade should be turned to the left. Line up all the pieces carefully, and clamp them to the work surface. (Place the clamp in the middle of the top case piece).

7. With your brace and a 1/4" bit, carefully bore two holes at the two marks on the top case piece, through all three pieces. The hole for holding the blade is centered on the top face, near the right end of the case. The other hole is lower on the top face, near the left end.

8. Next, use your marking tools, clamp, and coping saw to cut two 3-4"-long pieces of 1/4" dowel.

9. Sand all three knife pieces with 100- and 150-grit sandpaper, and wipe the sawdust off.

10. Now, with your 1/2" paintbrush, apply two coats of silver paint to the blade and to the case pieces' inside faces. Let the pieces dry well before you handle them again.

11. Stack the three pieces together. Holding the stack tightly in one hand, put a small drop of glue (just a bit) into each side of each hole.

12. Set the stack flat on your work surface, and use your hammer to tap a dowel into each hole until it's even with the top face. Wipe off the glue and pick up the knife. The blade should fold in and out of the case easily. If it doesn't, ask your adult helper for help adjusting it. Then set the knife aside until the glue dries.

13. If the dowel ends stick out of the case, sand them lightly with 150-grit sandpaper. Wipe every speck of sawdust off.

14. If your adult helper has a real pocket knife, get some help carving the small slit in the blade; you can see it in the photograph. Though it isn't really necessary, this slit will let you slip the blade out of the case with your fingernail.

15. The knife in the photograph is painted in traditional colors, but you can paint yours anyway you choose. When the paint has dried, show your pocket knife off, but remember that it's just for play!

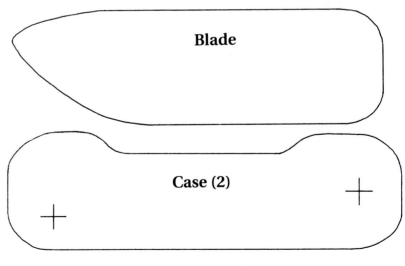

+ = hole location

◆③ Doll's Cradle

Your favorite doll will be a sleeping beauty in this handmade rocking cradle.

MATERIALS

1   Scrap 1 x 10, at least 20" long
6   3/8" x 36" dowels
    3d finishing nails
    Wood glue
    Sandpaper, 100-grit and 150-grit
    A piece of thin string, about 8" long
    A small pie pan, or a similar, circular object,
      between 7-1/2" and 8" in diameter
    Stain, your choice of color
    Varnish
    A stick for stirring
    Mineral spirits or turpentine
    1" paintbrush
    Rags and newspapers

TOOLS

Marking tools   Coping saw
C-clamp   Brace with 3/8" bit
Handsaw   Rasp
Hammer

CUT LIST

1   9-1/4"-diameter circle (cut from 1 x 10 scrap)   Headboard
1   9-1/4"-diameter circle (cut from 1 x 10 scrap   Footboard
      and then cut in half)
12 3/8" dowels, each 16" long   Stretchers

PUTTING IT TOGETHER

1. Set the piece of 1 x 10 flat on your work surface. Use your marking tools, clamp, and handsaw to cut the board to a length of 20".

2. Before you can cut circles from this board, you'll need to draw a center line along its length. To do this, measure and mark two or three points, each 4-5/8" from one long edge. Then use your pencil and a straight scrap of wood as a ruler to draw a line that runs through all these points.

3. Next, measure 4-5/8" from one end of the board, and square across the mark. Hammer a 3d finishing nail lightly into the point where the two lines meet.

4. First, read "Measuring and Marking Circles" on page 74.

Then, using those instructions, draw a circle on the 1 x 10. Tie your string to the 3d nail, and adjust the string's length so that your pencil point touches down where the 4-5/8" line ends at the 1 x 10's edge.

5. Repeat Steps 3 and 4 to draw another circle at the other end of the 1 x 10.

6. Using your clamp and a coping saw, cut out the two circles. To keep your sawing hand from getting tired, clamp the board upright on your work surface. This may not be possible if your work surface is an old table, but it will be if you've built the workbench (in "Part Three"). Hold the coping saw firmly, and keep the blade straight as it cuts the line.

7. Clamp one circle flat on your work surface, and cut along the line that you drew in Step 2. One of the half-circles that you've just cut will be your cradle's footboard. (Put the other half-circle in your scrap bin.) The full circle will be the cradle's headboard.

8. Use the clamp and your rasp to smooth the edges of the footboard and headboard. Try to smooth out all of the saw marks, and use your eyes to tell you if part of an edge is "out of round." If you clamp the footboard and headboard together so that their edges match, you can rasp them both at once.

9. Have an adult friend help you with the next few steps if you get confused. Set the cradle's footboard flat on your work surface

with its rounded edge closest to you. Set the pie pan (or another circular object) onto the footboard so that there's approximately 1/2" between the footboard's round edge and the edge of the pan. With your pencil, draw a line around the pan's edge onto the wood.

10. Hook your tape measure over the footboard's straight edge, along the line you just drew, and mark the curved line at 1/2". Then, starting at the 1/2" mark, make five more marks along the curved line, each 1" apart. Because the line is curved, you'll have to take each measurement from the mark you made last; you can't leave the tape measure's hooked end on the footboard's straight edge because the tape won't bend.

11. Starting at the other end of the curved line, repeat Step 10 to make one 1/2" mark and five more 1" marks. You should now have twelve marks on the curved line.

12. Set the footboard on top of the headboard, and then set both pieces on top of a piece of scrap wood on your work surface. Line up the circular edges and the grain lines of the footboard and headboard, and clamp all three pieces to your work surface.

13. With your brace and a 3/8" bit, bore twelve holes through the marks you've made, right through both pieces. Be careful not to bore right through the scrap wood too!

14. Use your marking tools, clamp, and handsaw to cut twelve 3/8" dowel stretchers, each 16" long.

15. To make the heart-shaped hole in the headboard, set the headboard flat on your work surface with the holes you drilled closest to you and the nail hole facing up. Have an adult friend help you to measure and mark the top center of the headboard—the point on its edge that is farthest away from the holes you drilled. Use a straight scrap of wood to line up this mark with the nail hole, and then draw a line between them.

16. Measure and mark a point 2" from the top center mark, right on this line. Now draw a heart shape, about 2" tall and 2" wide, using

Measuring and Drawing Circles

To find the *diameter* of a circular object such as a bowl, just measure across the circle from edge to edge. The diameter measurements of any circle will be the same no matter which edges you use when you take them. You may have learned in school that one-half of this measurement (from the very center of any circle to its edge) is called the *radius*. And the *circumference* is the measurement around the circle's outside.

Here's an easy way to draw a circle on a piece of wood. Start a small nail in the center of the circle. Tie one end of a piece of string to the nail and the other end to a pencil. Holding the pencil straight up and down, and keeping the string stretched fairly tight, move the pencil around the nail. Be careful not to let the string slip up or down on the nail or the pencil as you're drawing.

the mark that you just made as the heart's center. Erase or sand off your pencil lines until you've drawn a heart that you like.

17. Clamp the headboard, with a piece of scrap wood under it, onto your work surface, and use your brace and a 3/8" bit to bore a hole just inside the heart shape.

18. Cut out the heart shape with your coping saw.

19. Rasp the inside of the heart shape until it's smooth.

20. Sand all parts of the cradle well with 100-grit and 150-grit sandpaper. Wipe off the sawdust carefully.

21. To assemble your doll's cradle, put a couple of drops of glue into each hole in the footboard, and slide or tap the twelve stretchers into the holes so that their ends are even with the footboard's outside face. Repeat this step to glue and insert the stretchers' other ends into the headboard's twelve holes. (You may need some help getting all twelve stretchers to go in!) Wipe up any excess glue that drips from the holes, and set the cradle aside while the glue dries.

22. This is a good project to stain and varnish. Brush or wipe the stain on carefully, and let it dry before you brush on the varnish. Two coats of varnish are always better than one!

23. A small doll's pillow (about 4" x 6") and a doll's blanket (or a crib blanket folded twice) will keep your doll cozy through those long nights!

◈ Bike Rack

You can be sure that your bike and all your gear will be safe once you put them on your own bike rack.

MATERIALS

1 Scrap 1 x 8, at least 18" long
1 Scrap 1 x 6, at least 42" long
1 Scrap 3/8" dowel, at least 9" long
4 3/8" x 2-1/2" lag bolts with washers
10 No. 10 x 1-1/2" flathead wood screws
     6d finishing nails
     Wood glue
     Sandpaper, 100-grit and 150-grit
     A jar lid, about 6" in diameter
     A piece of a wax candle
     Varnish
     A stick for stirring
     Mineral spirits or turpentine
     1" paintbrush
     Rags and newspapers

TOOLS

Marking tools	Screwdriver
C-clamp	Coping saw
Handsaw	Brace with 3/8" and 1" bits
Hammer	Rasp
Twist drill with 5/32" bit	

CUT LIST

1	1 x 6 x 18"	Back
2	1 x 6 x 12"	Supports
1	1 x 8 x 18"	Shelf
3	3/8" dowels, each 3" long	Pegs

PUTTING IT TOGETHER

1. Use your marking tools, clamp, and handsaw to cut the pieces in the Cut List.

2. Set one of the 12"-long supports flat on your work surface. At one end, use your tape measure and pencil to measure and mark a point on the face, 4-1/2" from the edge. At the other end, measuring from the same edge, mark the same face at 3". With your pencil and a straight scrap of wood, connect the two points with a line.

3. Use your clamp and a handsaw to cut the line you drew.

4. Repeat Steps 2 and 3 to cut the other support.

5. Next, set the jar lid flat on one support's top face, at the 3"-wide end. Position it so that its curved edge lines up with both the corner of the edge that you didn't cut and the edge that you did cut. With your pencil (and using the jar lid's edge), draw a curved line that connects the support's two edges.

6. Use your clamp and a coping saw to carefully cut the curved line you made.

7. Repeat Steps 5 and 6 to mark and cut another curved line on the other support piece.

8. You might need a hand from an adult helper as you take the next three steps. Place a piece of scrap wood on your work surface, and then set both supports flat on the scrap. Press the two uncut edges of the supports together, with their 3"-wide ends at the same end. Now clamp the pieces to your work surface, putting the clamp's metal pad onto the joint where the two edges meet and close to the 3" ends. The clamp pad should hold both pieces tightly to the work surface.

9. Measure and mark the joint, 2" from the 3" clamped end.

10. With your brace and a 1" bit, bore a hole right through the joint at the 2" mark. Have your adult helper make sure that the two support pieces don't shift, and keep the brace and bit straight up and down as you bore the hole. When you take the support pieces apart, each one should have a half-hole.

11. To mark the back and shelf for boring, look carefully at the illustrations of these pieces. The measurements for the four screw holes in the back are given in the upper left-hand corner. The measurements for the four bolt holes are given in the upper right-hand corner. The measurements for the three peg holes are given in the lower left-hand corner and underneath the illustration. Do have your adult helper give you a hand with measuring and marking!

12. Now bore the marked holes. You'll need to use a twist drill and 5/32" bit, as well as your brace and a 3/8" bit to bore them.

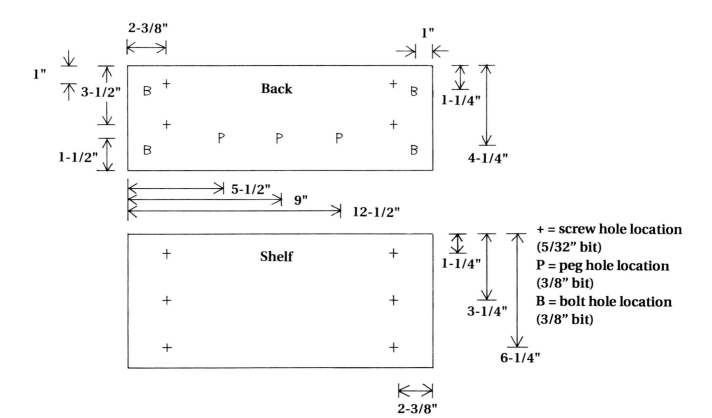

2-3/8"

1"

1"

3-1/2"

1-1/2"

B +   **Back**   + B

+   +

B   B

P   P   P

1-1/4"

4-1/4"

5-1/2"

9"

12-1/2"

+   **Shelf**   +

+   +

+   +

1-1/4"

3-1/4"

6-1/4"

2-3/8"

+ = screw hole location
(5/32" bit)

P = peg hole location
(3/8" bit)

B = bolt hole location
(3/8" bit)

Check the illustration to make sure that you're using the right bit for each hole. Be sure to protect your work surface by putting a scrap piece under your work before you bore the holes.

13. Before you sand the pieces, use your rasp to smooth the curved cuts that you made with your coping saw. Then carefully sand all the parts with 100- and 150-grit sandpaper, and wipe all the sawdust off.

14. You'll probably need some help assembling your bike rack, so go ahead and ask for it! Using the assembly illustration as a guide, first run glue lines on the support pieces' wide ends. Then use your screwdriver to attach them to the back (through the 5/32" holes) with No. 10 x 1-1/2" screws. The supports' top edges (with the half-circles in them) should be even with the back's top edge (the edge farthest away from the five 3/8" holes). Make sure the screws go into the middle of each support's end. To start the screws, rub a little candle wax onto their threads, and then tap them lightly with a hammer.

15. Now set the assembly on your work surface with the back's bottom edge facing down, and the half-circles on the supports facing up. Run a line of glue along the back's top edge and about 6" out towards the ends of both support pieces. Keep the glue lines about 3" away from the half-circles. Set the shelf onto the gluey edges so that its back edge lines up with the back's outside face. Then drive a screw into each of the holes you bored so that the shelf fits tightly onto the gluey edges.

16. Now put a drop or two of glue into each 3/8" peg hole that you bored, and push or tap a 3/8" x 3" peg into each hole.

17. Using 100- and 150-grit sandpaper, sand all the parts of your bike rack carefully. Wipe the sawdust off, and then finish the rack with two coats of varnish.

18. Mount your bike rack with lag bolts and washers on a stud wall or plywood wall. The four bolt holes that you bored earlier are marked with the letter B in the illustration. Ask your adult helper for a hand doing this. Then store your bike and gear away!

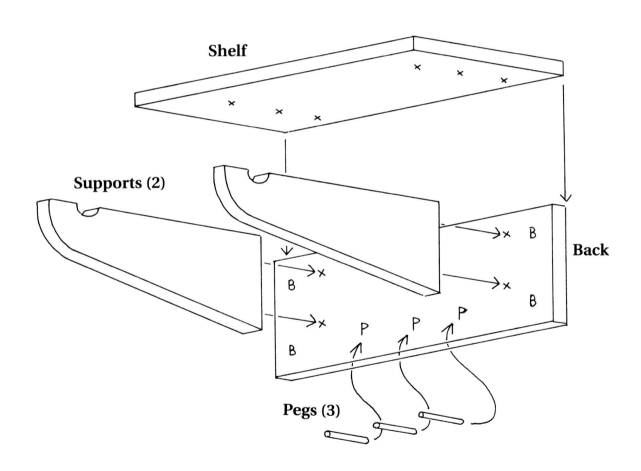

Shelf

Supports (2)

Back

Pegs (3)

Hat Tricks and High-Sticking

To play hockey, you'll need a friend who enjoys games as much as you do. Place the hockey set on a sturdy, low table or flat on the floor. Put the two pins in their holes, and choose which end you want to defend.

To start, a player sets the puck anywhere on his or her end zone, and hits it with the hockey stick, trying to knock down the other player's pin at the far end. The defending player protects that pin with the hockey stick. After the first hit, the defending player gets a turn, hitting the puck from wherever it came to rest. Each player takes one shot at a time, until a pin is knocked over and a goal is scored. No player can hit the puck if it's on the other player's end zone; the player whose zone the puck is in gets to strike it again until it's outside the colored area.

A *hat trick* (three goals) means a winner. In this game, *high-sticking* is shooting the puck so hard that it flies above the hockey set's surface—and it's not allowed! Good luck!

20. Clamp the 1 x 4 to your work surface, and carefully cut out the circle shape with your coping saw. This is your hockey puck. If it isn't quite round, round up its edges with your rasp.

21. Carefully sand all the parts of your hockey set, starting with 100-grit sandpaper and finishing up with 150-grit sandpaper. Set the two dowel pins in their holes to be sure that they'll stand up; if they're wobbly and fall over, sand the bottom of each hole until it's flat. Wipe off all the sawdust.

22. Use your 1" paintbrush to paint one end zone, one hockey stick, and one pin with one color. Paint the other end zone, stick, and pin with a contrasting color, and paint the puck black. (Don't forget to rinse out your paintbrush well between colors.) When the first coat of paint is dry, add another coat and let it dry. Now you're ready to play!

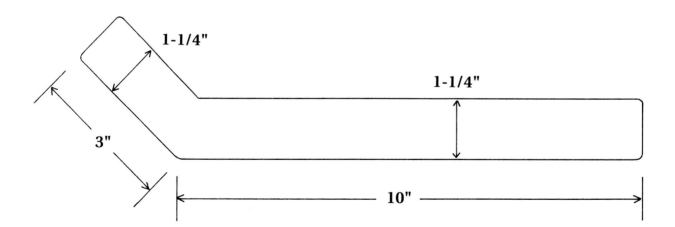

FOR YOUR ROOM

◆ Display Cabinet

Exhibit your special things in a handmade cabinet that's as good-looking as what's on display.

MATERIALS

1	1 x 4 x 12'
4	2-1/2" corner braces with screws
	4d finishing nails
	Wood glue
	Sandpaper, 100-grit and 150-grit
	Masking tape
	Stain, any color
	Varnish
	A stick for stirring
	Mineral spirits or turpentine
	1" paintbrush
	Rags and newspapers

HINTS!

When you buy the corner braces and screws, ask the salesperson what size drill bit you should use to drill the screw-holes. Check to see that your screwdriver is the right size for these smaller screws. If it isn't, borrow or buy the right tool for the job.

If you've got enough scrap, you may not need to buy the 1 x 4 x 12.

TOOLS

Marking tools	Twist drill with 1/8" bit
C-clamp	Screwdriver
Handsaw	Rasp
Hammer	

CUT LIST

2	1 x 4 x 22-1/4"	Sides
2	1 x 4 x 18"	Top and bottom
2	1 x 4 x 16-1/2"	Shelves
1	1 x 4 x 10-3/4"	Shelf
2	1 x 4 x 5"	Shelves

PUTTING IT TOGETHER

1. Use your marking tools, clamp, and handsaw to measure, mark, and cut the nine pieces in the Cut List. Have a friend support the 12' 1 x 4 as you cut. Be sure that your cuts are square.

2. Using the illustration as a guide, glue the 18" top and 18" bottom to the ends of the 22-1/4" sides to form a box shape. With your hammer, drive 4d finishing nails through the faces of the top and bottom and into the ends of the sides. Check to see that the box's corners are square.

3. To assemble the shelves, you'll first need to mark them. Rest the box shape on your work surface—on its edges. Then check the illustration to see where each piece belongs. Arrange the five shelves inside the box, moving them around until they're all squared and in place. Then use your pencil to mark the shelves where they touch each other. Also mark the inside of the box wherever the shelves touch it.

4. Take the shelves out. Then glue and nail the two 16-1/2" shelves to each other. Use the lines you've drawn to position one shelf's end against the other shelf's face.

5. Now glue and nail on the two 5" shelves and the 10-3/4" shelf.

6. Set this assembly back inside the box. If it doesn't fit easily, use your rasp to remove a little wood from the end of any board that is sticking out. Do try to keep the boards' ends nice and square.

7. When everything fits well, put a thin line of glue on every end of the shelf assembly (there should be six lines of glue). Slide the assembly down into the box.

8. Line up all the shelves with the marks you made. Then hammer a couple of 4d finishing nails through the box's outside face, into each end of the shelf assembly. You'll find that it's easier to drive these nails if you stand the box upright.

9. You might need a hand from your adult helper as you complete the next few steps. Set the cabinet on its front edges. Then place a corner brace on the edges of each back corner. With your pencil, mark the location of each hole in the four braces. Remove the braces.

10. Now get out your twist drill and a 1/8" bit (or whatever size bit the salesperson recommended). Make a flag to mark a 1/2" depth by wrapping a piece of tape around the bit. Then bore a 1/2"-deep hole into each of the brace-hole positions that you marked with your pencil. Be sure to stop boring when the flag touches the wood!

11. Set the braces back on the corners, and use your screwdriver to drive the screws through the brace's holes.

12. Sand your display cabinet well, starting with 100-grit paper and then using 150-grit paper for a really smooth surface. Wipe the sawdust off.

13. For the finishing touch, stain your cabinet with a color you like, and when the stain is dry, add two coats of varnish. Let the finish dry well.

14. Set your cabinet on a table, desk, or chest of drawers. Turn it onto any side you like. Before you decide which side should face up, experiment by arranging your things in it.

15. If you want to hang your display cabinet on a wall, get some help from an adult and from the salesperson at the hardware store so that you'll hang it just right.

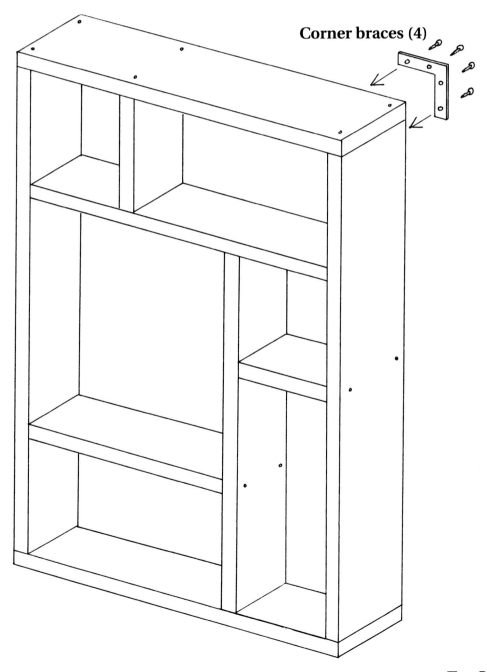

Corner braces (4)

♦ Desktop Bookshelf

Can't you find those important books? Build this attractive organizer, and your problem will disappear.

MATERIALS

1   Scrap 1 x 8, at least 36" long
1   Scrap 1 x 4, at least 24" long
    4d finishing nails
    Wood glue
    Sandpaper, 100-grit and 150-grit
    Varnish
    A stick for stirring
    Mineral spirits or turpentine
    1" paintbrush
    Rags and newspapers

TOOLS

Marking tools   Handsaw
C-clamp   Hammer

CUT LIST

2	1 x 8, angled from 9" to 10" in length	Sides
1	1 x 8 x 10-1/2"	Back
1	1 x 4 x 10-1/2"	Support
1	1 x 4 x 12"	Front

PUTTING IT TOGETHER

1. Set the 1 x 8 flat on your work surface, and check one end for square. If that end isn't square, use your marking tools, clamp, and handsaw to square it.

2. Hook your tape measure over the squared end, close to one edge, and measure 19". With your pencil, mark that point on the edge. Then use your square to mark a line across the board at that point.

3. Now clamp the 1 x 8 to your work surface, and cut the marked line with your handsaw.

4. Take the 19" length that you just cut, and hook your tape mea-sure over one end. Measuring from that end, as close to one edge as you can get, mark with your pencil at 9".

5. Now move your tape measure down the board's end so that its hook is close to the board's other edge. Then measure and mark a point 10" from the end. Again, make your mark as close to the edge as you can.

6. Next, use a straight piece of scrap wood and your pencil to draw a line across the board's face, connecting these two points. The line should be angled, not square.

7. Clamp the marked 1 x 8 to your work surface, and cut along the line with your handsaw. You've just made the two sides; each has an angled bottom end.

8. Next, use your marking tools, clamp, and handsaw to square and cut the 1 x 8 x 10-1/2" back, the 1 x 4 x 10-1/2" support, and the 1 x 4 x 12" front.

9. Set the support on edge on your work surface, and run a line of glue along its top edge.

10. Set the back's face flat on top of the support's gluey edge so that the back's edge lines up with the support's face. Have a helper hold the two pieces in position for you.

11. Use your hammer to drive several 4d finishing nails through the back and into the support. If you bend a nail or drive one out the side of a piece, just pull the bent nail out, and drive a new one in another spot!

12. Have an adult helper give you a hand with this step if you have trouble figuring it out. Set the L-shaped back-and-support assembly on one end, and run a line of glue along the top end, right around the L-shape. Set the face of a side piece onto the gluey end, lining up its short (9") edge with the back's outside face, and its square end with the back's long edge. The support will hold up the side while you hammer a few 4d finishing nails into the joint; space these nails about 3" apart. Be sure to hammer a nail or two through the side and into the support, too.

13. Turn the assembly over so that it rests flat on the side piece,

and run a line of glue on the top end. Set the other side onto the gluey end so that it matches the first side. Line up the edges and ends, and hammer in a few 4d finishing nails.

14. Now turn the assembly over so that its back rests flat on your work surface; the two angled ends of the side pieces should face you. Run a 3" line of glue on the sides' two top edges, starting from the corners nearest to you. Set the front piece flat onto the gluey edges so that the front's two ends line up with the two sides' outside faces; the corners nearest to you should also line up exactly.

15. With your hammer, drive a couple of 4d finishing nails through the front and into the sides' edges.

16. Wipe up any glue spills, and carefully sand the assembly. Start with 100-grit sandpaper, and finish with 150-grit. Wipe away the sawdust when you're through.

17. Use your 1" paintbrush to apply two coats of varnish to your bookshelf, letting the varnish dry well between coats. When the varnish is completely dry, load the shelf with the books that you read most often!

Pages from Ancient History

You probably know that a book's pages are made from wood, but do you know how? First, logs are trucked to a giant paper mill. There they are ground up with water into a stew called *pulp*, cooked for a while, and then washed. Next, they're shaped and dried into sheets or rolls, and finally they're made into pages just like the one you're reading now.

How was paper made before we built paper mills? With great difficulty and loving care! *Cellulose*, a natural raw material that is a part of wood, grows over much of the earth in many different forms. Throughout the ages, people have experimented with cellulose in an effort to produce a thin, flat, strong, but inexpensive substance on which to write. Making paper usually involved beating pieces of trees, shrubs, and other plant parts into small fragments, heating them in water, pouring the mess out to form sheets, and letting the sun bake them dry. Sound familiar? The process may have been primitive, but it had all the ingredients of modern paper-making.

A lot of these handmade "papers of wood" didn't work very well; they were difficult and time-consuming to make, and their surfaces were very uneven. But two types of paper that were used by people thousands of years ago are still being made today!

One of the oldest known forms of paper is *papyrus*; in fact, the English word *paper* is based on the word papyrus. Long ago, in Egypt's Nile River valley, a type of tall reed called *Cyperus papyrus* was harvested and sliced very thinly, pounded flat, and soaked in water for a while. Strong paper was made from this material by first pressing several layers of it together at right angles to one another, and then leaving the layers in the sun to dry. Papyrus is still being made today,

just as it was when the great Pyramids were new, but you'll have a hard time finding it at your local market!

Mexican bark paper, produced by the Otomi Indians in Mexico, is the oldest paper known in the Americas. It was made long before the first Europeans arrived in the New World. Today, the Otomi still produce this beautiful paper in the traditional way. In the spring, the bark from certain local trees is collected and washed in a stream. Next, the bark is boiled in limewater (leftover from cooking corn) until its fibers soften. The fibrous "soup" is then poured onto flat boards and beaten to form sheets of paper. The hot sun does the rest of the work. Otomi paper is so highly prized that it's used by artists to make one-of-a-kind books and works of art.

Baseball Hold-All

Batter up!

MATERIALS

1   Scrap 1 x 6, at least 12" long
1   Scrap 1 x 4, at least 12" long
1   Scrap 1 x 2, at least 12" long
1   Scrap 3/8" dowel, at least 8" long
     4d and 6d finishing nails
     Wood glue
     Sandpaper, 100-grit
     Varnish
     A stick for stirring
     Mineral spirits or turpentine
     1/2" and 1" paintbrushes
     Rags and newspapers

TOOLS

Marking tools   Coping saw
C-clamp   Brace with 3/8" and 1" bit
Handsaw   Rasp
Hammer

CUT LIST

1   1 x 6 x 12"   Back
1   1 x 4 x 12"   Rack
1   1 x 2 x 12"   Support
2   3/8" x 4" dowel pieces   Pegs

PUTTING IT TOGETHER

1. Use your marking tools, clamp, and handsaw to square and cut the first three pieces of wood on the Cut List.

2. Set the 1 x 4 rack flat on your work surface. Draw a center line along the length of its top face (the line will be 1-3/4" from either long edge). Measuring from one end of this line, make pencil marks on it at 1-1/2" and 5".

3. Next, clamp the rack, with a scrap piece under it, to your work surface.

4. Using your brace and a 1" bit, bore holes through both of the marks you made.

5. Now hook your tape measure over the rack's edge, near the end that's farthest from the holes you bored. Measuring across the rack's face, make two marks with your pencil, at 1-1/4" and 2-3/4".

6. Press your try square's handle against the rack's end—the end that is farthest from the holes. Now line up the try square's blade with one of the marks you just made, and mark a 5"-long pencil line from the rack's end through one of the marks; use the blade as a ruler. Make another 5"-long, squared line through the other mark. Use your measuring tape to check that both lines are exactly 5" long. Then draw a line that connects the 5" ends of these two parallel lines.

7. Clamp the rack to your work surface. With your coping saw, cut out the 1-1/2" x 5" shape that you marked. If you round the two inside corners as you cut, instead

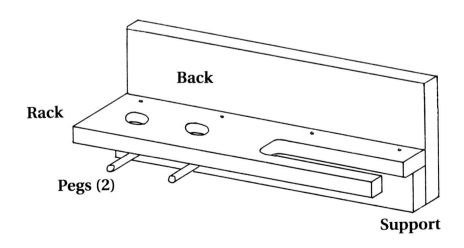

of trying to turn the saw blade sharply, sawing will be easier.

8. Next, set the 1 x 2 support on edge on your work surface, and put a line of glue along the top edge.

9. Have a helper hold the support steady. Find the long edge of the rack that has 1-1/4" of wood remaining between it and the cutout area you made. Then, lining up this long edge with the support's back face, set the rack's face onto the support's gluey edge. The ends of both pieces should be even.

10. While your helper steadies the two pieces, use your hammer to drive several 4d finishing nails through the rack's face and into the support's edge. Space these nails evenly.

11. Turn the assembly over so that the nailed-up rack edge faces up. Run a line of glue along this rack edge and along the support's face, too.

12. While your helper holds the assembly, set the 1 x 6 back down onto the gluey edge and face so that one of the back's long edges lines up with the support's bottom edge (the edge that isn't glued to the rack). Make sure that all the ends are lined up, too. Hammer several 6d finishing nails through the back, into the rack. Be careful to drive the nails straight in, and don't drive them near the holes in the rack.

13. Put a piece of scrap wood flat on your work surface, and then turn the assembly over, and set the back flat on the scrap. Clamp the pieces to the work surface.

14. On the support, measure and mark two points; these should be 1" down from the rack and in line

with each hole that you drilled in the rack.

15. With your brace and a 3/8" bit, bore two holes through the support and right through the back. Hold your brace and bit very straight!

16. Using your marking tools, a miter box or bench hook, and your handsaw, cut two 4" pieces of 3/8" dowel. Put a couple of drops of glue into each of the support's holes, and then push or tap the dowel pegs into the holes until they bump against the scrap beneath.

17. When the glue dries, carefully sand all the pieces. Use a rasp to smooth the rack's cutout, and finish up with sandpaper.

18. If you want to finish your project, carefully apply two coats of varnish. Let the project dry well.

19. To mount your project to a wall or to a solid wood door, get an adult helper to give you a hand with drilling holes in the hold-all and picking out the right hardware. Your friends at the hardware store can help you find what you need; show them your project, and tell them how you made it!

Making the Louisville Slugger

The world's most famous baseball bats have been made near Louisville, Kentucky, by the Hillerich and Bradsby Company for over one hundred and eight years. Today, though many bats are made of aluminum, more than one million wooden ones leave this factory each year, headed for countless contests on hundreds of noisy ball fields. As you can imagine, metal baseball bats come rolling out of machines like cookies from a cookie cutter, but how are wooden bats made?

The Louisville Slugger begins as a 3" x 40" *billet* (a skinny piece of rough wood) cut from a white ash tree. This wood has just the right properties for a great baseball bat: it's strong, light in weight, and has a springy "bounce" that can send a baseball over an outfielder's head! The billets are dried in a hot-air kiln for six weeks and are then sorted by weight and quality. A small number of the very best billets are set aside for a special purpose, as you'll see.

Almost all wooden bats are *turned* (or carved) on semi-automatic *lathes* (pronounced like bathes), machines which do just about all the work by themselves. These lathes use heavy, sharp cutters to shape each bat to a standard pattern; they turn out bats as quickly as the workers can put the wood onto them! Not all Louisville Sluggers, however, are made this quickly or easily.

Every year, around four thousand very special bats (made from those special billets) are turned by highly skilled people working at hand-turning lathes that are set apart from the rest of the machines. These bats are custom-made for ball players in the major leagues. Each one is carefully turned to the player's specifications; the finished bat is just the right weight and length for the player,

and its handle thickness fits his grip perfectly. Sometimes, a player will come to the factory to watch his bats being made and will take a few practice swings to make sure that his special-ordered bats are just right.

These days, the average major league baseball bat weighs around 34 ounces and is no longer than 34". The great Babe Ruth used a gigantic 42-ounce bat, but today's batters face trickier pitchers than the ones who played in The Babe's time; they need lighter bats so that they can swing quickly to match the curves and sliders coming their way. The maximum length for a Little League bat is 31"—enough lumber to send your baseball over the far fence with a loud crack!

 **Study Partner**

This project will brace your heavy textbooks while you study, and it acts as a mini-desk too.

MATERIALS

1   Scrap 2 x 4, at least 18" long
1   Scrap 1 x 12, at least 18" long
1   Scrap 1 x 8, at least 18" long
1   Scrap 1 x 4, at least 18" long
2   1" dowels, at least 36" long
12 No. 10 x 1-1/2" flathead wood screws
    6d finishing nails
    Wood glue
    Sandpaper, 100-grit and 150-grit
    Varnish
    A stick for stirring
    Mineral spirits or turpentine
    1" paintbrush
    Rags and newspapers

TOOLS

Marking tools   Hammer
C-clamp   Twist drill with 5/32" bit
Handsaw   Screwdriver

CUT LIST

1   2 x 4 x 18"   Desktop support
1   1 x 12 x 18"   Desktop
1   1 x 8 x 18"   Book support
1   1 x 4 x 18"   Back
4   1" dowels, at least 18" long

PUTTING IT TOGETHER

1. Use your marking tools, clamp, and handsaw to cut all the pieces in the Cut List. If you can't remember how to square a wide board, read page 21. And if you've built a miter box, use it when you saw the dowels!

2. Clamp one 18" dowel "flat" to your work surface, with a piece of scrap wood sandwiched between. Use your tape measure to measure 1", 9", and 17" from one end of the dowel; use your pencil to mark each point along the dowel's top.

3. Now use your hammer and a nail to dimple each of the three marks you made.

4. With your twist drill and a 5/32" bit, bore three holes in the three marks that you made. While you bore, keep the drill straight up and down.

5. Repeat Steps 2, 3, and 4 to mark and bore the other three dowels.

6. Carefully sand all the pieces with 100- and 150- grit sandpaper, and wipe the sawdust off.

7. While you helper holds the desktop on edge, set a bored dowel onto the edge that faces up. Line up the desktop's ends with the dowel's ends, and make sure that the dowel's holes are facing up. Your helper can hold the dowel steady while you start three No. 10 x 1-1/2" flathead screws through the holes and into the desktop's edge. Tap the screws with your hammer, making sure they go into the center of the desktop's edge, and then drive them all the way in with a screwdriver. If you can't drive the tops of the screws even with the wood, have your helper give you a hand.

8. Turn the desktop over, and repeat Step 7 to fasten a dowel to the other edge.

9. Repeat Steps 7 and 8 to screw two bored dowels onto the two edges of the back piece.

10. Set the desktop support flat on your work surface, and run two lines of glue from one end of its top face to the other end, spacing them about 2" apart. Set the desktop onto the gluey desktop support so that one edge of the desktop lines up exactly with one edge of the support, and the ends of both boards match. One dowel should hang over the edge of the support.

11. Turn the pieces over, and

have a helper hold them in position while you hammer eight 6d finishing nails through the support and into the desktop. Space the nails in two rows, with the nails in each row about 5" apart.

12. Now run two lines of glue on the desktop support's top face. Set the book support onto the gluey desktop support so that one edge of the book support lines up exactly with the desktop support edge that's farthest from the overhanging dowel.

13. While your helper steadies the assembly, hammer eight 6d finishing nails through the book support and into the desktop support. Use the same nailing pattern as you did in Step 11.

14. Now set the back flat on your work surface. It will sit up a little on its dowel edges. Using the illustration as a guide, and measuring from one edge near an end, use your pencil to mark at 2-3/4" on the back's face. Make another mark on the other end of

the face, measuring the same distance from the same edge. Then connect the two lines, using your pencil and a straight scrap of wood.

15. Turn the desktop assembly so that the desktop's face is facing you, and the edge of the desktop support rests on the edge of the work surface. Then run a line of glue along the book support's top edge.

16. Set the back onto the book support's gluey edge so that the line you made lines up exactly with the

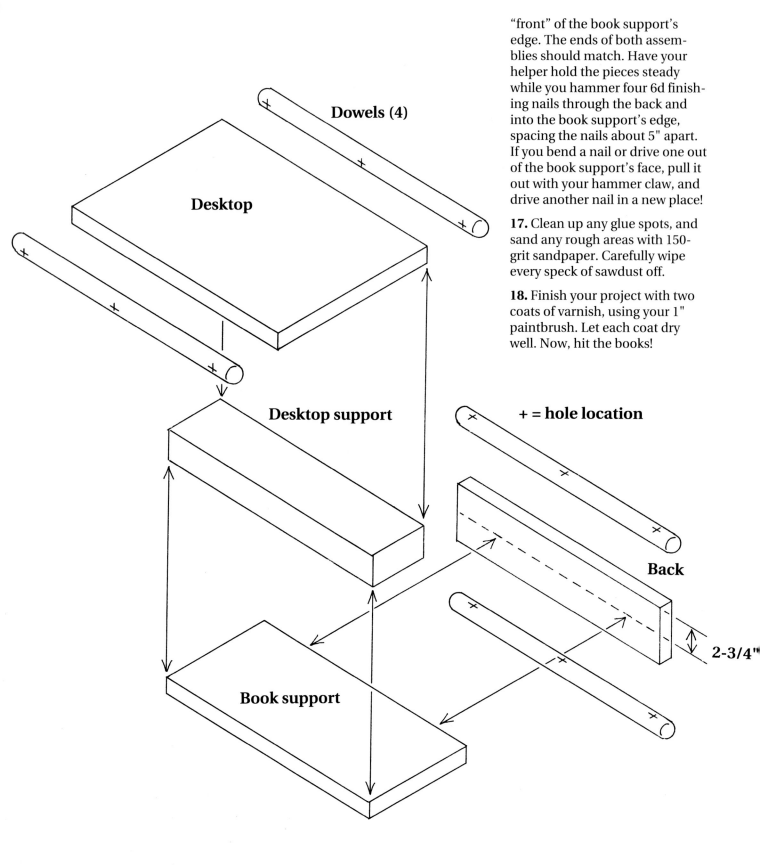

Dowels (4)

Desktop

Desktop support

Book support

Back

+ = hole location

2-3/4"

"front" of the book support's edge. The ends of both assemblies should match. Have your helper hold the pieces steady while you hammer four 6d finishing nails through the back and into the book support's edge, spacing the nails about 5" apart. If you bend a nail or drive one out of the book support's face, pull it out with your hammer claw, and drive another nail in a new place!

17. Clean up any glue spots, and sand any rough areas with 150-grit sandpaper. Carefully wipe every speck of sawdust off.

18. Finish your project with two coats of varnish, using your 1" paintbrush. Let each coat dry well. Now, hit the books!

Modular Shelf Unit

This handy shelf unit keeps your belongings just where you want them. You can hang it up on a wall, or you can build several units and stack them to make a bookcase.

MATERIALS

For each unit:

1   Scrap 1 x 10, at least 48" long
1   Scrap 1 x 8, at least 30" long
     6d finishing nails
     Wood glue
     Sandpaper, 100-grit and 150-grit
     Varnish
     A stick for stirring
     Mineral spirits or turpentine
     1" paintbrush
     Rags and newspapers

TOOLS

Marking tools   Handsaw
C-clamp   Hammer

CUT LIST

For each unit:

1	1 x 10 x 28-1/2"	**Back**
2	1 x 10 x exactly as long as your 1 x 10 is wide	**Sides**
1	1 x 8 x 28-1/2"	**Shelf**

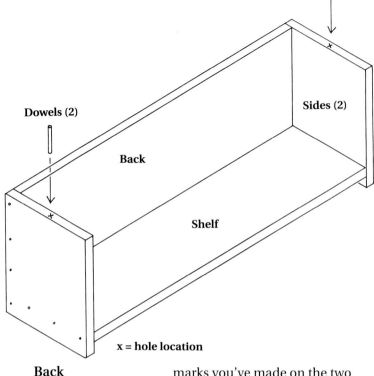

Dowels (2)

Back

Sides (2)

Shelf

x = hole location

PUTTING IT TOGETHER

1. Set the 1 x 10 on your work surface. Then, using your clamp, marking tools, and handsaw, cut the 28-1/2"-long back.

2. The two side pieces should be exactly as long as the 1 x 10 is wide, so before you cut them, measure the 1 x 10's width. Then cut the two sides; each one will be as long as the measurement you just took (probably around 9-1/4").

3. Clamp, measure, and cut a 28-1/2"-long shelf from the 1 x 8.

4. Have a helper hold the back so that it stands upright, with one end on the ground. Put some glue on the top end, and set the face of a side piece on the gluey end so that the side's end lines up with the back's face, and the edges on both pieces line up evenly. (The wood grain of both pieces should run in the same direction.)

5. While your friend holds the two pieces together, hammer several 6d finishing nails through the side and into the back.

6. Next, turn the nailed pieces over. Then glue and nail the other side onto the back.

7. Set the assembly on your work surface; place it on its edges, with its open section facing you. Using a pencil and measuring down from the top edge of one side, make several 1" marks along that side's inside face. Mark the inside of the other side's face in the same way.

8. Have your friend hold the shelf on one edge. Then run a line of glue along the edge and ends that are showing. Next, set the assembly down onto the shelf very carefully so that the shelf lines up at both ends with the

marks you've made on the two sides. There should be a 1" space between the sides' ends and one face of the shelf.

9. Hammer evenly spaced 6d finishing nails through the back, into the shelf's edge. If you aren't sure where to put the nails, measure and mark along the back's outside, just as you did earlier on the inside of each side, and then use the marks as guides for your nails.

10. Now turn the shelf unit onto one end, and hammer several nails through one side and into the shelf. Be sure that the shelf lines up with the marks you've made! Turn the shelf unit over, and nail through the other side and into the shelf.

11. Carefully sand and dust off your shelf unit.

12. Finish your project with two coats of varnish. Let it dry well, and then have a parent or older friend help you hang it on your wall. Now load up your special things!

Modular Stacking Bookshelf

MATERIALS

1   Scrap 3/8" dowel
    Masking tape
    Wood glue
    Sandpaper, 100-grit and 150-grit
    A piece of wax candle

TOOLS

Marking tools   Hammer
Handsaw   Brace with 3/8" bit

Pieces of furniture that fit together to make larger pieces (or that come apart when you want to store them) are called *modular* pieces. A modular chair, for instance, works well by itself, but it can also be put together with many other chairs so that a lot of people can sit together. You've probably seen modular seating at bus stations or airports.

Your shelf unit can be hung on a wall, of course, but it can also be stacked with other units to make a modular bookshelf that rests on the floor. To build your bookshelf, first make two or three shelf units. (Don't try to put more than three together!) The units are then attached to each other with dowels. To make the dowel holes and assemble the units, just follow the instructions that come next.

PUTTING IT TOGETHER

1. On the floor or on your work surface, stack the units on top of each other. Line up their edges very carefully.

2. From either outside corner of the stack, measure 5" along the line where two sides meet each other. Mark this point carefully on both sides.

3. Measure and mark 5" points at all the other places where two sides meet. If you have two units, you'll be marking two points (one on each side). If you have three units, you'll mark four points (two on each side).

4. Then take the units apart, and set the bottom unit on the work surface with its open part facing you.

5. Hold your try square so that the blade lies across the top edge of one side and lines up with the mark you made. Then mark a pencil line across the side's edge.

6. Now measure 3/8" across that line, and mark an X. This X should be at the very center of the side's edge.

7. For every mark you made (on all the units), repeat Steps 5 and 6.

8. Using your brace and a flagged 3/8" bit, carefully bore a 1-1/2"-deep hole into each X mark. Hold the brace straight! You don't need to bore holes into the top of your highest unit or into the very bottom of your lowest unit because nothing will attach to these surfaces.

9. Cut a 3/8" x 2-1/2" dowel for each pair of matching holes that you bored (two dowels for two shelves or four dowels for three shelves).

10. Put a drop or two of glue onto one end of a dowel piece, and hammer it into one of the holes on a top edge (not on a bottom edge) of a shelf unit. Be sure to clean up any extra glue with a rag.

11. Repeat Step 10 for all the holes on the top edges.

12. Carefully sand the dowels so that they're rounded at the top.

13. Dust the dowels off, and rub a little candle wax onto each one. The wax helps them fit easily into the other holes that you bored.

14. When the glue dries, you're ready to assemble your shelves. Just rest one unit on top of the next; the dowels will fit into the holes on the shelf above them. Stack your shelves, and then stack your books!

Thumbs-Up Coat Rack

This hand-y hanger will tickle your friends.

MATERIALS

For a single hanger:

1   Scrap 1 x 6, at least 9" long
1   Scrap 1 x 4, at least 9" long
2   No. 10 x 1-1/2" flathead wood screws
2   Mounting screws
    3d finishing nails
    A pair of scissors
    Wood glue
    Sandpaper, 100-grit and 150-grit
    Finishing materials, your choice

HINTS!

You'll need to go to your local photocopy shop and get two, enlarged copies of the illustration. Ask for help making these copies.

Show your completed project to someone at the hardware store, and ask for help picking out your mounting screws. Get an adult helper to give you a hand mounting your coat rack, too.

TOOLS

Marking tools   Twist drill with 5/32" bit
C-clamp   Screwdriver
Handsaw   Coping saw
Hammer   Rasp

PUTTING IT TOGETHER

1. Use your scissors to cut out the entire hand shape (including the fingers) from one copy of the illustration. Cut the smaller finger shape (without the hand) from the other copy. Mark the paper cutouts so that you know which side is "face-up" after you cut them out!

2. Set the two shapes (face up) on your 1 x 6 so that the wood grain runs up and down in the same direction as the raised thumb on the large shape. The grain on the smaller shape should run across the fingers. Then use your pencil to trace around both shapes' edges, onto the wood.

3. Clamp the 1 x 6 to your work surface, and carefully cut out the hand and finger shapes with your coping saw, stopping whenever you need to loosen the saw's handle and adjust the blade.

4. Spread some glue on the back of the fingers cutout, and then place the fingers on the hand cutout. Now hammer a couple of 3d finishing nails through the fingers cutout to complete the hand shape.

5. Clamp the hand shape to your work surface, and use your rasp and sandpaper to smooth all the edges and surfaces. The knuckles on both pieces should be nice and even.

6. Use your marking tools, clamp, and handsaw to square and cut a 1 x 4 piece that is 9" long.

7. With your marking tools, draw a line down the center of the 1 x 4's length. (This line should be 1-3/4" from either long edge.)

8. Next, measuring from one end of the center line, mark small Xs with your pencil at 3/4", 2", 4", and 8-1/4".

9. Clamp the 9" board, with a scrap piece under it, to your work surface. Dimple the four X marks with your hammer and a nail, and then use your twist drill and a 5/32" bit to bore through all four marks.

10. Carefully sand the 9" piece.

11. Clamp the hand shape to your work surface with its flat sleeve facing up. Run a line of glue along the sleeve's top edge.

12. Set the 9" piece down onto the gluey sleeve so that the two center holes (the ones you marked at 2" and 4") are lined up exactly with the sleeve's center. Have a helper hold the two pieces together while you use your hammer to start two No. 10 x 1-1/2" flathead wood screws through the holes and into the sleeve. Finish driving these screws in with your screwdriver.

13. Clean up any glue spills, wipe

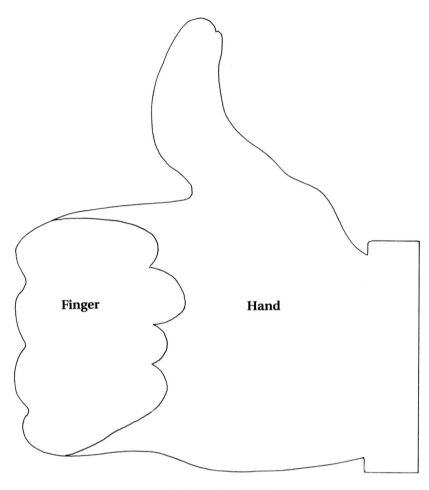

Finger

Hand

Enlarge by 125 %

the sawdust off your coat rack, and finish it in any way that you like. Get an adult helper to help as you attach it to a wall or solid wood door. Then hang up your coat, and give yourself a hand!

TO MAKE A LARGER COAT RACK

Three hand shapes can be screwed vertically onto a horizontal 1 x 4 x 18" board, which is then mounted on a wall or door. This project takes a little longer, of course! You'll need all the materials listed for the smaller version of

the coat rack, but make sure that your 1 x 6 is at least 27" long, your 1 x 4 is at least 18" long, and that you have six flathead wood screws instead of two. Bore mounting holes 1" from either end of the board, and position the hand shapes so that they're spaced equally along the board.

Audio-Visual Storage Cube

*You'll enjoy keeping your compact discs, cassettes,
and video cartridges in this revolving storage cube.*

MATERIALS

1   Scrap 1 x 10, at least 30" long
1   Scrap 1 x 4, at least 36" long
1   Scrap 1" dowel, at least 10-1/4" long
17   No. 10 x 1-1/2" flathead wood screws
   3d finishing nails
   Wood glue
   Sandpaper, 100-grit and 150-grit
   Masking tape
   A piece of wax candle
   Varnish
   A stick for stirring
   Mineral spirits or turpentine
   1" paintbrush
   Rags and newspapers

TOOLS

Marking tools	Twist drill with 5/32" bit
C-clamp	Screwdriver
Handsaw	Brace with 1" bit
Hammer	Rasp

CUT LIST

3	1 x 10 x 9-1/4"	Top, bottom, and base
4	1 x 4 x 7-3/4"	Sides
1	1 x 4 x 3-1/2"	Collar
1	1" dowel, 10-1/4" long	Rod

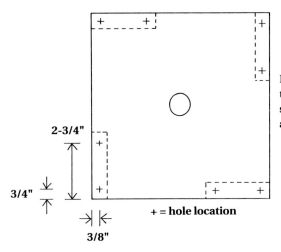

2-3/4"

3/4"

3/8"

Location of the ends of the 1 x 4 side pieces and screw-holes on both top and bottom of cube

+ = hole location

PUTTING IT TOGETHER

1. Using your marking tools, clamp, and handsaw, cut the nine pieces in the Cut List.

2. To find the exact center of one of the 1 x 10 x 9-1/4" pieces, place a straight scrap of wood diagonally so that it runs from one corner of the 1 x 10 to the opposite corner. Then, using the scrap as a ruler, mark a line along the 1 x 10 with a pencil. Use the scrap again to mark another line between the other two corners. The two lines should look like the letter X; they'll cross at the board's center.

3. Repeat Step 2 to find the centers of the other two 1 x 10 pieces and of the collar.

4. Now clamp a marked 1 x 10 piece, with a piece of scrap wood under it and its marked side up, to your work surface.

5. With your brace and a 1" bit, bore a hole through the board's center. This will be the cube's bottom.

6. Clamp another marked 1 x 10 piece (the cube's top) and piece of scrap wood onto the work surface. Flag the 1" bit with a piece of masking tape, 3/8" from the bit's cutters (not from the bit's screw-tip). Bore a 3/8"-deep hole in the top's center; if you stop boring as soon as the tape touches the wood, your hole will be exactly the right depth!

7. Repeat Step 6 with the third 1 x 10 piece (the base).

8. Clamp the collar, with a piece of scrap under it, to your work surface, and bore a 1" hole at the center mark, all the way through the board.

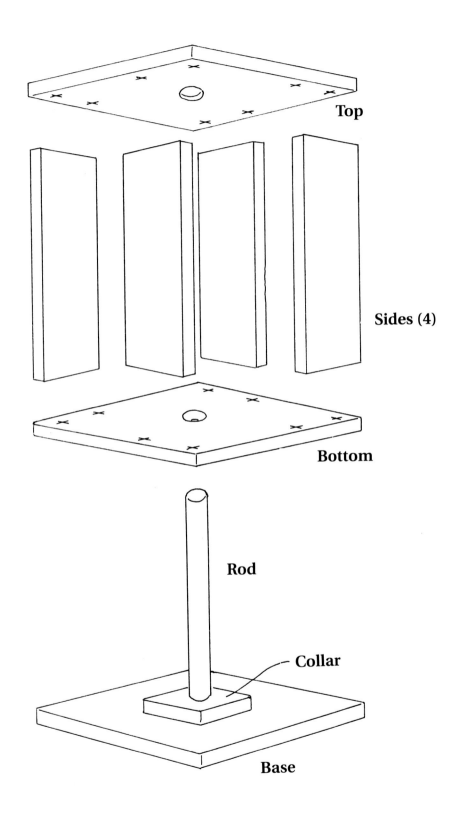

Top

Sides (4)

Bottom

Rod

Collar

Base

9. Put a little glue on one face of the collar, and set the gluey face down onto the center of the base. The two holes should line up exactly.

10. Hammer four 3d finishing nails through the collar's corners, into the base.

11. Turn the glued-up assembly over, and find the center by marking the base's bottom face with diagonal lines (see Step 2).

12. Use your twist drill and a 5/32" bit to bore a pilot hole through the base's center.

13. Turn the assembly over again, and put a little glue into the 1" hole.

14. Set the dowel rod firmly into the bottom of the gluey hole. Tap the dowel with your hammer if necessary.

15. Turn the pieces over once again, and have a friend hold them together while you use your screwdriver to drive a No. 10 x 1-1/2" screw through the small hole you drilled and right into the dowel. (Start the screw by tapping it into the dowel with your hammer.) Set the assembly aside to dry.

16. With your twist drill and 5/32" bit, and using the illustration as a guide, drill eight pilot holes in the bottom and top pieces.

17. Have a helper give you a hand setting up the top, sides, and bottom on your work surface; the illustration shows how they fit together. While your helper holds the pieces in place, use your screwdriver to assemble the cube. Drive the screws through the pilot holes until they rest *flush* (flat) with the face of the top or bottom piece.

18. Set the glued-up dowel assembly flat on your work surface, with the dowel facing up. Then place the cube onto the dowel so that the bottom drops over the rod and the rod's top end fits into the hole in the top. If the rod doesn't fit easily through one hole and into the other, rasp or sand a bit of wood from the two holes.

19. Test the assembly by turning the cube on the dowel. Then take the cube off, and carefully sand all the parts until they're smooth. Start with 100-grit paper, and finish with 150-grit. Wipe the sawdust off.

20. Now take the cube off the dowel assembly. To protect the wood, give both parts of the storage cube a couple of coats of varnish. Be careful not to let any varnish drip into the holes, though, and don't put too much onto the dowel; you don't want the dowel to stick in the holes! When the two parts are dry, you can reassemble them. A little candle wax rubbed onto the dowel's top end now and then will keep the cube turning smoothly.

21. Load your cassettes and compact discs flat into the openings in the cube; video cartridges load vertically. Your audio-video storage cube will hold either 44 cassettes, 72 compact discs, or 16 video cartridges. Of course, you can put some of each in your storage cube if you wish!

ANIMAL FRIENDS

◈ ① Throw Bone

If your pooch likes to chase and retrieve sticks, he'll love this project!

MATERIALS

1   Scrap 2 x 4, at least 10" long
1   Scrap 1" dowel, at least 9" long
     6d finishing nails
     Sandpaper, 100-grit

HINT!

Use untreated lumber for this project, and don't put a
    finish on it. Wood preservatives and finishes aren't
    good for your dog's health.

TOOLS

Marking tools   Hammer
C-clamp   Brace with 1" bit
Handsaw

CUT LIST

2   2 x 4 x 3-1/2"   Sides
1   1" x 9" dowel   Bite-bar

PUTTING IT TOGETHER

1. Use your marking tools, clamp, and handsaw to cut two 3-1/2"-long side pieces from the 2 x 4. Make those cuts nice and straight!

2. Measure, mark, and cut a 9" bite-bar from the 1" dowel; use your clamp (or a miter box or bench hook) to secure the dowel before you saw it.

3. Set one of the sides flat on your work surface, and find the exact center of its top face by drawing two diagonal lines, one between each set of opposite corners. The lines will cross at the side's center.

4. Clamp the side, with a piece of scrap wood under it, to your work surface, and use your brace and a 1" bit to bore a hole right through its marked center. Focus on keeping your brace and bit straight as you bore this hole.

5. Repeat Steps 3 and 4 to mark and then bore the other side piece.

6. Sand all three pieces well, using 100-grit sandpaper.

7. Slide one of the sides onto the bite-bar so that 3/4" of the bar pokes out past the side's face. You may need to tap the side with your hammer as you do this.

8. Place the other side on the bar's other end. Your project should now look like one of the barbells that weight-lifters use.

9. Set the assembly on your work surface with the two sides on edge. Then hammer a 6d finishing nail through the center of one side's top edge, right into the bite-bar. Do the same thing to one edge on the other side. Now roll the assembly toward you once so that two new edges are on top. Hammer two more 6d finishing nails into the dowel through those edges. These nails will keep the assembly tight.

10. Double-check that all the edges are sanded well. Wipe the project off, and throw it for your dog. You'll both have fun!

House Mouse

Your kitty will pounce on this playful mouse!

MATERIALS

1   Scrap 1 x 12, at least 12" long
1   Scrap 1 x 4, at least 10" long
1   1" dowel, 36" long
1   No. 8 x 1-1/2" round-head (or flathead) screw
    3d finishing nails
    Masking tape
    Wood glue
    Sandpaper, 100-grit and 150-grit
    A piece of heavy string, 32" long
    A piece of tracing paper
    A piece of carbon paper
    Latex enamel paint, grey and black, or your favorite colors
    A stick for stirring
    1/2" paintbrush
    Rags and newspapers

TOOLS

Marking tools   Twist drill with 1/8" and 5/32" bits
C-clamp   Screwdriver
Handsaw   Coping saw
Hammer   Brace with 1" bit

CUT LIST

1   1 x 12 x 11-3/8"   Base
1   1 x 4 x 3-1/2"   Collar
1   1" dowel, 30" long   Post
1   1" dowel, 6" long   Arm

Dashes show location for 5/32" hole

PUTTING IT TOGETHER

1. Use your marking tools, clamp, and handsaw to cut the four pieces on the Cut List. Set them aside when you're through.

2. Set the scrap of 1 x 4 (left over from cutting the collar) flat on your work surface. Trace the mouse shape in the illustration onto the wood. (If you can't remember how to do this, see page 36.)

3. Clamp the scrap 1 x 4 to your work surface, and use your coping saw to cut out the mouse shape. You'll probably need to remove and re-clamp the scrap as you saw out the shape.

4. Use your hammer and a sharp nail to dimple the mouse's back. (The illustration shows the location.)

5. Re-clamp the mouse flat on the work surface, with its back facing out toward you, and use your twist drill and a 5/32" bit to bore a hole through the dimple, right through the mouse. Hold the twist drill so that it's level with the ground.

6. Next, set the base flat onto your work surface, and use a straight scrap of wood and your pencil to mark two diagonal lines on its face, from corner to corner. The lines will cross in the base's center.

7. Now put some glue on one face of the collar, and set the gluey face down onto the base's center so that the collar's corners line up with the lines on the base.

of wood underneath the arm.

15. Use your tape measure and a pencil to make two marks on the arm's top side, 1" in from each end.

16. Use your hammer and a sharp nail to dimple both marks. Then use your twist drill and a 5/32" bit to bore through each dimple, right through the arm.

17. Set the arm on the dowel post's top end so that the hole in the arm lines up with the center of the post's top end. Use your screwdriver to drive a No. 8 x 1-1/2" screw through the hole and into the dowel post. (If you have trouble driving the screw, bore a 3/4"-deep pilot hole in the end of the clamped post with your twist drill and a 1/8" drill bit first.) Drive the screw tightly!

18. Double-knot one end of the string, and push the other end through the top of the second hole in the arm piece. Push it through the bottom of the hole, using a small piece of wire if you need to. Pull the string through until the knot is tight against the top of the hole.

19. Push the string's bottom end through the hole in the mouse's back until it pokes out from the mouse's tummy. Knot the string under the mouse's tummy so that 6" is left over to form the mouse's tail.

20. Now paint your mouse grey, with black edges, or use your favorite colors. Set it where your kitty can reach it, and watch the fun!

8. Use your hammer to drive a 3d finishing nail down through the collar and into the base, near one of the collar's corners. Then drive 3d finishing nails near the other three corners.

9. Clamp the base-and-collar assembly flat on your work surface, with the collar facing up.

10. Use your pencil and a straight scrap of wood to find the collar's center, just as you did with the base in Step 6.

11. Use your brace and a 1" bit (flagged for a 1" depth) to bore a hole into the center of the base-and-collar assembly. Stop boring when the flag touches the wood.

12. Put some glue into the hole you bored, making sure that the glue goes on the hole's sides.

13. Push or tap the dowel post into the gluey hole until it touches bottom. Then set the assembly aside until the glue has dried.

14. Clamp the dowel arm "flat" on your work surface with a scrap

◇② **Bird Box**
Build a house for the new bird in your neighborhood!

MATERIALS

1   Scrap 1 x 8, at least 7-1/4" long
1   Scrap 1 x 6, at least 26" long
1   Scrap 1 x 4, at least 18" long
2   8d galvanized common nails
    No. 17 x 3/4" brads
    3d, 4d, and 6d finishing nails
    Wood glue
    Sandpaper, 100-grit and 150-grit
    Masking tape
    Exterior varnish
    A stick for stirring
    Mineral spirits or turpentine
    1" paintbrush
    Rags and newspapers

TOOLS

Marking tools	Hammer
C-clamp	Twist drill with 5/32" bit
Handsaw	Brace with 3/8" bit

CUT LIST

1   1 x 8 x 7-1/4"   Top
1   1 x 6 x 6"   Back
1   1 x 6 x 4-13/16"   Bottom
2   1 x 6, cut with an angle so that one edge is   Sides
    6" long, and the other edge is 7-1/4" long
1   1 x 4 x 12"   Long support
1   1 x 4 x 4"   Short support
1   3/8" dowel, 7-1/4" long Perch

PUTTING IT TOGETHER

1. Use your marking tools, clamp, and handsaw to cut the eight pieces in the Cut List. To cut the two angled side pieces, first square and saw a 1 x 6 exactly 13-1/4" long. Then make a mark on one edge, 6" from one end. Mark the other edge 7-1/4" from the same end. Connect the two marks across the 1 x 6's face, using a pencil and a straight scrap of wood as a ruler. Next, clamp the piece and cut it with a handsaw.

The two pieces of 1 x 6 will be the sides. Be sure to label all pieces as you cut them so that you won't get confused when you put them together!

2. Line up one angled side evenly on top of the other side, and place them flat on your work surface.

3. To drill a hole for the perch, first hook your tape measure over the top face's square end (not its angled end). Then measure 2" along the top face, close to the 7-1/4" edge, and make a mark with your pencil. The mark should be about 1/2" from the edge.

4. Now sandwich a piece of scrap wood between the stacked sides and your work surface, and clamp the three pieces down tightly.

5. With your brace and a 3/8" bit, bore a hole through both sides, right at the mark you made. Don't bore through the scrap wood!

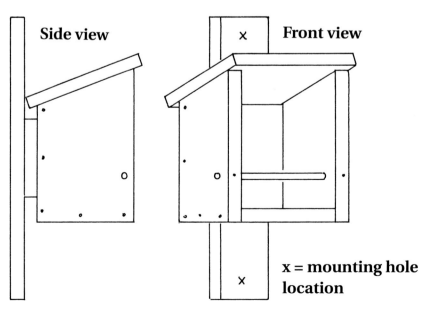

Side view

Front view

x = mounting hole location

6. Have a helper hold the back on edge on your work surface, and run a line of glue along the back's top edge, from one end to the other.

7. Set an angled side onto the gluey surface so that its 6" edge is even with the back's face, and the ends on both pieces are even. The two pieces should form a right angle.

8. While your helper holds the pieces steady, use your hammer to drive three 4d finishing nails through the side and into the back. The nails should be evenly spaced and about 2-1/2" apart.

9. Repeat Steps 6, 7, and 8 to glue and nail the other side onto the back's other edge. Your nailed assembly should look like the letter U.

10. Run a thin line of glue down both edges and one end of the bottom. Slide it into the squared end of the U-shaped assembly. The gluey sides and end should fit snugly into the assembly.

11. Turn the assembly so that you can secure the bottom to it by driving a couple of 4d finishing nails into each side.

12. Turn the assembly onto its back, and slide the perch through both the holes in the sides. Pin the perch's ends into the sides by hammering a brad through each side's edge, right into the perch.

13. Now turn the assembly onto its bottom, and set the top onto it; the top's grain should run in the same direction as the bottom's grain. Let the top hang 1" over the sides' front edges, and line up its two edges with the sides' outer faces.

14. Use your hammer to drive a few 4d finishing nails through the top and into the assembly. (You don't need to glue on the top.)

15. Turn the bird box onto its top, and then clamp the top to your work surface.

16. Use your twist drill and a 5/32" bit to bore two holes through the back two corners of the bottom. These holes will let any water that blows into the bird box drain out.

17. Set the long support flat on your work surface, and use your tape measure and a pencil to mark 4" from one end, on the top face.

18. Put some glue on one face of the short support, and set it onto the long support so that one end of the short support lines up exactly with the 4" mark that you made.

19. Use your hammer to drive several 3d finishing nails through the short support's top face and into the long support.

20. Clamp the two supports to your work surface, with a scrap of wood sandwiched between the pieces and the surface.

21. With your twist drill and a 5/32" bit, bore two holes through the long support. Each hole should be 1" in from each end and centered on the long support (the center is at 1-3/4").

22. Turn the bird box so that the open front rests face down on your work surface.

23. Spread some glue on the short support's face, and set the nailed-together supports onto the box's back so that the gluey face is centered there. (Use your tape measure to center it carefully.)

24. Now use your hammer to drive four 6d finishing nails through the supports' backs into the back of box. Space the nails about 2-1/4" apart so that they make a square shape once you've finished hammering.

25. Sand your bird box well with 100-grit and 150-grit sandpaper, and wipe the sawdust off.

26. To protect your bird box from the weather, finish it with two coats of exterior varnish.

27. Use your hammer and the two 8d galvanized nails to hang your bird box on a wall or tree, facing north or north-east, 6' or 8' above the ground. Drive the nails through the two holes in the long support piece. Now watch for the first birds to move into their brand-new bird box!

Measurement A (outside
diameter of bowl + 1/4")

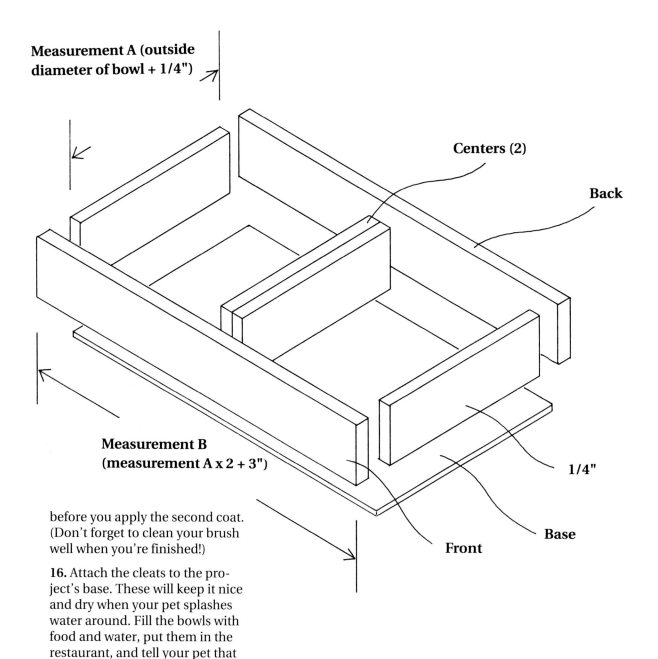

Centers (2)

Back

Measurement B
(measurement A x 2 + 3")

1/4"

Base

Front

before you apply the second coat.
(Don't forget to clean your brush
well when you're finished!)

16. Attach the cleats to the project's base. These will keep it nice
and dry when your pet splashes
water around. Fill the bowls with
food and water, put them in the
restaurant, and tell your pet that
dinner is served!

Come and Get It!

To make your pet's mealtime
really fun, spend a few minutes
personalizing his or her restaurant with your painting tools.

MATERIALS

Latex enamel paint
  (It should contrast with
  the color of the restaurant. On red, try blue or
  green; on yellow or blue,
  try red or orange.)
A stick for stirring
Detail paintbrush
Rags and newspapers

1. Using your pencil, lightly
draw a design, your pet's name,
or whatever you like onto the
restaurant.

2. Now use your detail paintbrush to apply as many colors of
paint as you wish. Clean up and
be sure to let the paint dry before
your pet arrives!

 # Pet Nest

When it's time for a snooze, what pet wouldn't love this comfy nest with its colorful wood-chip cushion?

HINT!

Because pets come in different sizes, you'll want to build a nest that's just right for your own favorite animal. With a tape measure, measure your standing pet along its back, from nose to rear end, but don't include the tail. Which size nest should you choose?

Small nest   All cats—and dogs under 24"

Large nest   Dogs over 24"

Yes, your pet pig will love its nest! But please, no flying squirrels or hippos.

MATERIALS

1   1 x 6, 8' or 10' long
1   Scrap 1/2"-thick plywood (See Cut Lists for sizes.)
     4d and 6d finishing nails
     Wood glue
     Sandpaper, 100-grit and 150-grit
     A jar lid, about 3" in diameter
     Latex enamel paint
     A stick for stirring
     1" paintbrush
     Rags and newspapers

TOOLS

Marking tools	Hammer
C-clamp	Coping saw
Handsaw	Rasp

CUT LIST (Small Nest)

1	1 x 6 x 24"	Back
2	1 x 6 x 16-1/2"	Sides
2	1 x 6 x 6"	Front
1	16-1/2" x 22-1/2" plywood	Floor

CUT LIST (Large Nest)

1	1 x 6 x 36"	Back
2	1 x 6 x 25-1/2"	Sides
2	1 x 6 x 10"	Front
1	25-1/2" x 34-1/2" plywood	Floor

PUTTING IT TOGETHER

1. Using your marking tools, clamp, and handsaw, cut the back, sides, and front for either the small or large nest.

2. Measure, mark, and cut the plywood floor to the right size. Get some help if you need it; sawing plywood is hard work!

3. Have your helper hold the floor upright, with one short edge facing up. Run a line of glue along that top edge, and then place the face of one side piece onto the gluey edge. The side's edge should line up with the floor's face. With your hammer, nail the side onto the floor's edge with several 4d finishing nails. Repeat this step with the other side, attaching it to the floor's other short edge.

4. Now have your helper hold the plywood floor so that one long edge is facing up. Put some glue on that edge, and on the ends of each side.

5. Nail the back onto the floor's gluey edge with 4d finishing nails; its ends should line up with the outside faces of the sides. Drive 6d finishing nails through the back, into the floor and into the sides' ends.

6. You don't want your pet to get hurt on the sharp corners of the two front pieces, so the next step is to round them off. Place a front on your work surface, and set your jar lid down on one of its corners. The lid's rounded edge should just touch the edge and the end in that corner. With your pencil, draw a curved line around the lid's edge, onto the wood. Do the same thing with the other front piece. Set the lid aside.

7. Clamp a front piece to your work surface, and then use your coping saw to cut around the curved line. Repeat this step with the other front piece. Then smooth the curved edges with your rasp.

8. Glue and nail the two front pieces to the last edge of the floor, one at each end. (You'll notice in the photograph that the space between these two pieces is the nest's entrance. The square corners of the front pieces are nailed, and the rounded corners face the entryway.) Now drive 6d finishing nails through each front piece into the sides' ends.

9. Sand all parts of the nest, and wipe off the sawdust.

10. Paint the nest with two coats of your pet's favorite color.

Built for Comfort!

For centuries, all kinds of critters have been sleeping on wood chips—even people. Not so long ago, before the modern inner-spring mattress was invented, whole families slept on handmade mattresses filled with carefully collected straw, corn shucks, or wood chips. You can make a wonderful wood-chip cushion for your pet.

HINT!

To find wood chips, try calling a cabinetmaker, who may be glad to have you pick some up. The telephone company or local street maintenance crew may have some too. Wood chips work much better than sawdust, and if you can get cedar chips or chips from some other strong-smelling wood, they'll help to keep fleas off your pet.

MATERIALS

Colorful, sturdy cloth rectangle, just as wide and twice as long as the inside of your nest
Sewing needle
Strong thread

PUTTING IT TOGETHER

1. Fold the cloth over itself so that the short ends meet.

2. Thread your needle with plenty of thread. If you've never sewn before, get help from someone with experience.

3. Sew the two edges of the cloth together almost all the way around, leaving about 12" unsewn. Use a running stitch.

4. Now fill the cloth cushion with wood chips. Add chips until the cushion is about 4" thick, but don't pack it so tightly that your pet will think it's a brick!

5. Sew up the remaining edge of the cushion. Put the cushion in the nest, and invite your pet over for a nap.

 Bird Buffet

Here's a dangling diner for twittering tweeters.

MATERIALS

1   Scrap 1 x 10, at least 24" long
1   3/4" dowel, 36" long
1   1/4" x 1-1/2" x 8' lattice
2   Screw hooks (see Hints!)
    Jack chain or heavy wire, at least 4'
    3d finishing nails
    No. 17 x 3/4" wire brads
    Wood glue
    Sandpaper, 100-grit and 150-grit
    Exterior latex enamel paint
    A stick for stirring
    1" paintbrush
    Newspapers and rags

HINTS!

If you can't find the 1/4"-thick lattice at your building supply
    store, try an arts supply store or frame shop.

Get screw hooks with shafts at least 1-1/2" long and no thicker
    than 3/16".

TOOLS

Marking tools   Screwdriver
C-clamp   Coping saw
Handsaw   Brace with 1/4" and 3/8" bit
Hammer

CUT LIST

2   1 x 10 x 9-1/4"   Roof and base
1   3/4" dowel, 16" long   Hanger
2   3/4" dowels, 10" long   Supports
4   1/4" x 1-1/2" x 9-1/4" lattice   Trim
4   1/4" x 1-1/2" x 9-3/4" lattice   Trim

PUTTING IT TOGETHER

1. Use your marking tools, clamp, and handsaw to cut the roof and base from the 1 x 10.

2. Set the roof on top of the base, with the grain of both pieces running in the same direction. Then set both pieces flat on a large scrap of wood, and clamp the stack to your work surface.

3. Use your marking tools to draw a line through the roof's center, from one end to the other.

(The center is 4-5/8" from the edge.)

4. Now, along the line you drew, measure 1" in from the end, and mark an X on the line. Measuring 1" from the other end of the line, mark another X on the line.

5. Using your brace and a 3/4" bit, bore two holes, one through each of the X marks, right through the roof and base. Don't bore through the scrap wood, though!

6. Use your marking tools and a coping saw (or a miter box or bench hook if you've made one, and a handsaw) to cut four 9-1/4"-long trim pieces from the lattice.

7. Have your helper hold the roof upright, with one 9-1/4" edge on the work surface. Put a thin line of glue along the top edge.

8. Now set the face of a trim piece on the glue line so that the trim piece's edge lines up with the roof's face, and the ends of both pieces are even.

9. Use your hammer to drive several brads through the trim and into the roof.

10. Turn the roof over so that the trim sits flat on the work surface. Then glue and nail another trim piece onto the roof's top edge.

11. Repeat Steps 8, 9, and 10 with the base and two more trim pieces.

12. Repeat Step 6 to cut four more trim pieces, but this time, make each piece 9-3/4" long.

13. With your helper, glue and nail the four trim pieces onto the

other edges of the roof and base to make two shallow trays. Be sure to line up all the ends and edges carefully before you nail them.

14. To keep the trim pieces tight, carefully hammer a brad through one of the longer trim pieces so that it goes right into the end of the trim piece next to it. Hammer brads into the other corners of the roof and base, too.

15. Use your marking tools and coping saw to cut two 10" supports and one 16" hanger from the 3/4" dowel.

16. Set the roof flat on your work surface so that the open part of the tray is face up. Press or tap the two supports into the 3/4" holes.

17. Now turn the roof and supports upside down. Use your hammer to tap the roof down

until exactly 1-1/2" of each support sticks out the roof's top.

18. To keep the supports tight, turn the roof so that you can hammer a 4d finishing nail through one trim piece and the end of the roof, into one of the supports. Then do the same thing to hammer another nail into the other trim piece, roof, and support.

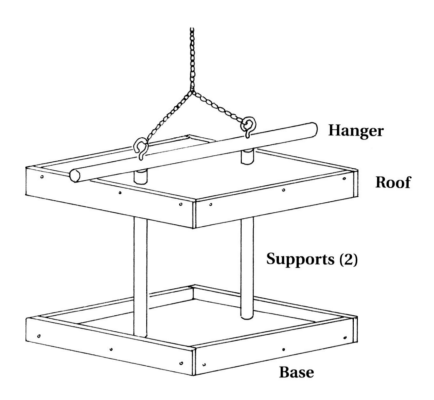

Hanger

Roof

Supports (2)

Base

19. Have your helper hold the pieces while you tap the base onto the supports' other ends. The roof and base should face each other. Tap the base until the supports' ends are even with the base's outside face.

20. Repeat Step 18 to hammer 4d finishing nails through the trim pieces and base into the two supports.

21. Set the base flat on your work surface. Rest the hanger on top of the two supports' ends, and center it with your tape measure so that the hanger extends past the two supports by the same amount.

22. Use your pencil to mark the hanger exactly where it sits on the center of each support.

23. Clamp the hanger to your work surface with a scrap of wood sandwiched between them, and the two marks facing up.

24. Use your hammer and a nail to dimple the hanger at both marks.

25. Use your brace and a 1/4" bit to bore holes through the dimples you made, right through the hanger.

26. Set the hanger back on the supports' ends, and use your hammer to lightly tap screw

hooks through the holes, into the center of the supports' ends, until the tips bite into them. Now use the screwdriver's shaft to turn the screw hooks down into the supports' ends until the hooks rest on the hanger. (The shaft will slip through the eye of the screw hook, giving you the leverage you need to turn it.)

27. Sand your bird buffet carefully, and wipe off the sawdust.

28. Apply two coats of exterior enamel paint to your project, and hang it high with a chain or wire so that cats can't reach it! Put some birdseed in the base—your feathered friends will love it!

GIFTS YOU CAN BUILD

 ## Place-Card Holders

Easy and fun to create, these place-card holders make great gifts for anyone who loves a party. You might want a few for your own parties, too!

MATERIALS

Several pieces of scrap wood, 3/4" thick
Sandpaper, 100-grit and 150-grit
Latex enamel paint, several colors
A stick for stirring
1/2" paintbrush
Rags and newspapers

TOOLS

Marking tools   Coping saw
C-clamp   Rasp
Handsaw

Holiday Holders

A set of place-card holders cut in special holiday shapes makes a gift that will be enjoyed for years. Select shapes that remind you of the holiday you've chosen: a turkey for Thanksgiving, a Santa or pine tree for Christmas, an egg or bunny for Easter, a dreidel or a little temple for Chanukah. You don't need to make your shapes very elaborate; it's surprising how easily we can recognize simple shapes for what they are.

PUTTING IT TOGETHER

1. Set a scrap piece face down on your work surface. With your pencil, sketch shapes that you like on the scrap's top face. Each shape should have one flat edge and should be about 2" across. Make sure that they're all roughly the same size so that they'll look good when they're grouped together on the party table. And sketch enough holders for everyone!

2. To cut out your shapes, clamp the scrap piece firmly. Use your handsaw to make the straight cuts and your coping saw to make the curved cuts. If you can't get to a straight line with your handsaw, cut it with the coping saw instead.

3. Once you've cut the holders out, clamp a holder to your work surface, with its top edge hanging over the surface's side. Then, with your coping saw, cut a slot 1/2" deep in the top of the holder; angle the cut just a little so that the place-card will slant backward in the finished cut. Cut one of these slots in every holder.

4. To remove any saw marks, first use your rasp, and then smooth all the rough edges by sanding each piece carefully. To sand the slots, just fold your sandpaper, and slide it down into them; then move the sandpaper back and forth.

5. Wipe the sawdust off all your pieces, and paint them as you like, trying not to get any paint in the slots. Let them dry really well. If you're going to give them away, wrap them up in colorful paper.

Picture Easel

Here's a grand stand for your works of art.

MATERIALS

1   Scrap 1/4" plywood, at least 9" x 9"
    Sandpaper, 100-grit and 150-grit
    Latex enamel paint in a color that you like
    A stick for stirring
    1" and 1/2" paintbrushes
    Rags and newspapers

TOOLS

Marking tools   Coping saw
C-clamp   Rasp
Handsaw

PUTTING IT TOGETHER

1. Clamp the plywood to your work surface. Then use your marking tools and handsaw to cut a 9" x 9"-square piece, turning and re-clamping the plywood as needed.

2. Have an adult friend help you with this step if you find it confusing! Begin by measuring and marking a point on one edge of the plywood piece, 3" from either end. Then turn the plywood around, and mark the opposite edge in exactly the same way.

Dotted lines indicate size of piece before it is cut.

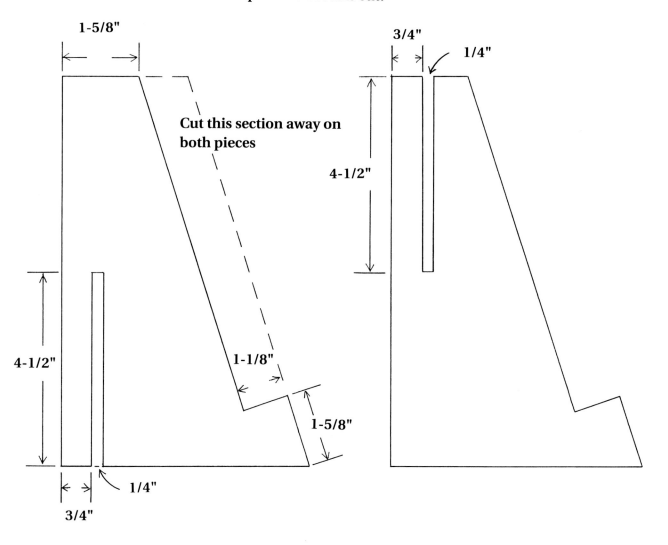

Cut this section away on both pieces

Next, rest a straight piece of scrap wood on the plywood's top face, and using it as a ruler, draw a line that connects the two marks on the edges. The line should run at an angle across the plywood.

3. Clamp the plywood onto your work surface, and cut the line with your handsaw. When you're finished, you'll have two matching plywood pieces, each shaped a little bit like a triangle.

4. Now refer to the illustration, and using it as a guide, draw cutting lines on the plywood pieces. Note that the 1/4"-wide cutouts are in different places on each piece! Clamp one piece to your work surface, and cut along the lines with your handsaw and coping saw. (Use the coping saw to make the small cut at the end of the 1/4"-wide cutout.) Clamp and cut the other piece in the same way.

5. Sand both pieces with 100-grit and 150-grit sandpaper, and wipe off any sawdust. Assemble the easel by sliding the two 1/4" cutouts all the way into each other until the easel will sit flat on your work surface. If the cutouts are too tight, sand or rasp away a little of the wood in the tight spots until everything fits together easily.

6. Take your easel apart, and apply two coats of your favorite color of paint. When the paint is dry, re-assemble the two pieces, and place your framed picture on the stand. Your picture easel can hold any frame that is smaller than 10" x 10" square.

Magazine Rack

This easy-to-build gift is perfect for parents or older friends. You might want to make one for yourself, too.

MATERIALS

1   Scrap 1 x 12, at least 32" long
    Sandpaper, 100-grit and 150-grit
    Varnish
    A stick for stirring
    Mineral spirits or turpentine
    1" paintbrush
    Rags and newspapers

TOOLS

Marking tools   Coping saw
C-clamp   Rasp
Handsaw

CUT LIST

2   1 x 12 x 16"   Sides

PUTTING IT TOGETHER

1. Use your marking tools, clamp, and handsaw to cut two 16"-long sides from the 1 x 12. Do you remember how to square a board that's wider than the blade of your try square is long? Mark one squared line first, then flip the handle of your try square to the opposite edge of the board, line the blade up with the squared line, and continue the line across the rest of the board.

2. Set a side piece flat on your work surface. From one end of this piece, measure and mark two points on the top face, one at 5" and one at 5-13/16"; both marks should be near the board's center.

3. From one edge of the piece, square and mark two lines across the top face, one through each of the two marks that you just made.

4. From the same edge, measure and mark a point 5-3/4" down, between the two lines. To connect the two lines, place the handle of your try square on the end of the piece that's nearest the lines, resting its blade on the 5-3/4" point, and then draw a line between the two marked lines.

5. Next, clamp the side to your work surface, and cut the two lines with your handsaw, right up to the short line that connects them. Tip the saw up at the end of each cut so that the cut will have a square end.

6. With your coping saw, cut along the short line that you drew. If the coping saw won't reach the cut, carefully snap the "tongue" out with your fingers instead, and sand the rough inside edge of the cutout with your rasp or sandpaper.

7. Repeat Steps 2-6 to cut the other side piece.

8. Slide the two cutouts together to check for fit. The two ends with 5" below the cutouts should match up, and the longer ends should be on top. Make sure that both sides' edges line up when the pieces are assembled. If the cutouts aren't deep enough to let the edges line up evenly, remove a little wood with either a rasp or sandpaper .

9. Carefully sand the two sides with 100-grit and 150-grit sandpaper, and wipe away the sawdust.

10. Finish your sides separately by applying a couple coats of varnish to each one. Remember to clean your brush really well when you're through. When the finish on both pieces is dry, assemble the rack (it doesn't need any nails), and surprise someone with it!

◆ **Trivet**

Got a hot pot or a favorite plant? This easy trivet's just the thing!

MATERIALS

1   Scrap 1 x 2, at least 18" long
3   3/8" dowels, each 36" long
     Wood glue
     Sandpaper, 100-grit and 150-grit
     Masking tape

TOOLS

Marking tools   Hammer
C-clamp   Coping saw
Handsaw   Brace with 3/8" bit

CUT LIST

2   1 x 2 x 9"   Sides
9   3/8" x 9" dowels   Rods

PUTTING IT TOGETHER

1. To cut one side piece, set the 1 x 2 on your work surface, and use your marking tools to square a line 9" from one end.

2. Use your clamp (or a bench hook or miter box if you've made one) to hold the piece firmly. Then cut the line with your handsaw.

3. Repeat Steps 1 and 2 to mark and cut a second side.

4. With your tape measure and pencil, measure across the face of one of the sides, and mark the center in a couple of places. If the 1 x 2 is 1-1/2" wide, the center of it is at 3/4". You may find that your board is a little wider than 1-1/2", so be sure to take its exact measurement and divide by 2 to get the halfway mark.

5. Next, use your pencil and a straight scrap of wood to draw a center line through the marks you've just made.

6. Measuring from one end through the center line, mark an X at 1/2". Then mark eight more Xs down the center line, each 1" apart.

7. Repeat Steps 4-6 to measure and mark the other side piece.

8. Secure a side to your work surface with your clamp.

9. Flag a 3/8" bit with a small piece of masking tape, wrapped 1/2" from the bit's cutters (not from its screw-tip).

10. Then, with your brace and the flagged bit, drill a hole into each X mark, stopping your drill as soon as the tape on the bit touches the side's surface. Clamp and drill the other side piece, too.

11. With your tape measure and a pencil, mark a 3/8" dowel at 9".

12. Holding the dowel firmly on your work surface (or in your miter box or bench hook), cut the line with your coping saw.

13. Measure, mark, and cut eight more 9"-long rods from the dowels.

14. Put a small drop of glue into each hole in one side piece.

15. Then press all nine rods into the holes; you may need to tap them lightly with a hammer.

16. Next, put a small drop of glue into the holes in the other side piece, and then carefully fit that piece over the other ends of the rods. Make sure the sides fit as tightly on the rods as possible, and then set the trivet on two edges to dry.

17. When the glue has dried, sand all the parts of your trivet. Wipe all the sawdust off before you give your trivet away!

② Key Caddy

This key-keeper will help someone you know to get organized!

MATERIALS

1	Scrap 1 x 4, at least 12" long
1	Scrap 1 x 2, at least 12" long
1	Scrap 1/4" dowel, at least 14" long
2	Small (1-1/8") screw eyes
	3d finishing nails
	Wood glue
	Sandpaper, 100-grit and 150-grit
	Masking tape
	String, wire, or ribbon, 10" long
	Varnish
	A stick for stirring
	Mineral spirits or turpentine
	1" and 1/2" paintbrushes
	Rags and newspapers

TOOLS

Marking tools	Screwdriver
C-clamp	Coping saw
Handsaw	Brace with 1/4" bit
Hammer	

CUT LIST

1	1 x 4 x 12"	Back
1	1 x 2 x 12"	Front
7	1/4" dowels, each 2" long	Posts

PUTTING IT TOGETHER

1. Use your marking tools, clamp, and handsaw to cut the front and back pieces. Check the ends of any board you use to be sure that the board is square. If it isn't, square it before you cut any project pieces from it!

2. Set the front on edge on your work surface. Next, you'll need to mark a line along the top edge's center, from one end to the other. First, measure 3/8" from either face, near one end of the piece, and make a pencil mark on the edge. Make another mark 3/8" from the face on the edge's other end. Then, using your pencil and a straight piece of scrap wood as a ruler, draw a line that runs through these two marks.

3. Now hook the end of your tape measure over one end of the top edge, and use your pencil to mark every 1-1/2" down the center line until you reach the other end. You should have seven marks along the center line.

4. Clamp the front to your work surface; the edge with the marks should be facing up. Tighten a 1/4" bit into your brace. Flag the bit with a small piece of masking tape, wrapped 3/4" above the bit's cutters (not above the screw-tip).

5. Bore seven holes, each 3/4" deep, at each of the marks that you've made, stopping each hole just as the masking-tape flag touches the wood. Hold the brace as straight as you can; try not to let it lean to the left or right, towards you or away from you.

6. Set the back piece flat on your work surface. Then run a line of glue on one face of the front piece, and carefully set it onto the back so that the edge without holes lines up with the back's bottom edge. Line up the corners too.

7. Use your hammer to drive two 3d finishing nails through the front's face and into the back; use one nail near each end. After you start each nail, hold the pieces together with one hand while you hold the hammer and drive the nail with the other.

8. Use your marking tools and a coping saw to cut seven 2"-long posts from the 1/4" dowel. The teeth on a handsaw are a bit too large to cut small dowels easily, so don't use your handsaw.

9. Set the assembly on your work surface so that the two glued-up edges are facing down, and the holes in the front are facing up. Put a drop of wood glue into each hole, and push the posts all the way in. You may need to tap them

with your hammer if they're tight.

10. After the glue has dried, carefully sand the key caddy (including the ends of each post) with 100-grit and 150-grit sandpaper. Wipe every speck of sawdust off.

11. With your brushes, apply two coats of varnish; use the 1/2" brush for the dowels. Let the caddy dry thoroughly.

12. Now use your hammer to start two small screw eyes into the back's top edge, about 3" in from each end. If you can, tighten the screw eyes with your fingers; if you can't, just slip a screwdriver tip through each screw eye, and turn the screwdriver to tighten the eye. Then tie the ends of the string, wire, or ribbon to the screw eyes, and give your handmade gift to someone who can't keep up with all those keys!

Crumb Box

This cutting box for bread will help any cook keep crumbs off the counter, and the birds will love the leftovers!

MATERIALS

1   Scrap 1 x 2, at least 42" long
1   Scrap 1/4" plywood, at least 9" x 13-1/2"
4   3/8" x 36" dowels
     No. 17 x 3/4" brads
     4d finishing nails
     Wood glue
     Sandpaper, 100-grit and 150-grit
     Masking tape
     Mineral oil
     A very clean rag

TOOLS

Marking tools   Hammer
C-clamp   Brace with 3/8" bit
Handsaw

CUT LIST

2   1 x 2 x 12"   Front and back
2   1 x 2 x 9"   Sides
1   1/4" x 9" x 13-1/2" plywood   Base
7   3/8" dowels, each 12-1/2" long   Rods

PUTTING IT TOGETHER

1. With your marking tools, clamp, and handsaw, cut the front, back, and side pieces. Then cut the seven rods. (Each of three 36" dowels will yield two 12-1/2" lengths, for a total of six rods; cut the seventh rod from the last 36" piece.)

2. Set a side piece flat on your work surface. Then measure down 3/4" from the top edge, and mark that point with your pencil. Do this in two more places along the side's face. Now draw a pencil line that runs through these three points by using a straight piece of scrap wood as a ruler.

3. Next, hook your tape measure over one end of the side, and use it to measure and mark every 3/4" on the center line that you just

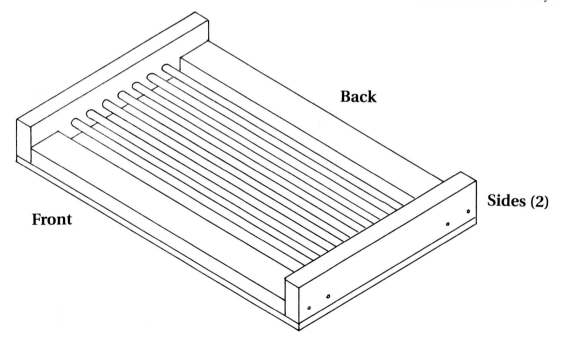

Back

Sides (2)

Front

drew, beginning at 2-1/4" and ending at 6-3/4". You should have seven marks right along the center line.

4. Repeat Steps 2 and 3 to measure and mark the other side piece.

5. Clamp one of the marked sides to your work surface, with the marks facing up. Wrap a piece of tape around a 3/8" bit, 5/16" from the bit's cutters (not from the bit's screw-tip). Next, use this bit and your brace to bore a 5/16"-deep hole at each of the seven marks. Don't forget to stop drilling as soon as the tape touches the wood!

6. Repeat Step 5 to bore seven holes in the other side piece.

7. Put a little glue on one end of the front piece. Have a helper hold it on the work surface with the gluey end facing up. Using the illustration as a guide, set one of the sides on the gluey front so that its holes face down and the corners are lined up exactly. Then hammer two 4d finishing nails through the side's face right into the gluey end of the front.

8. Repeat Step 7 to nail the same side piece onto the gluey back. The assembly should now be shaped like the letter U, with the bored holes inside the letter shape.

9. This step is a bit tricky, so use your helper! Set the assembly on your work surface with the side flat and the bored holes facing up. Put all seven dowels into the seven holes. You may need to tap them lightly with your hammer. Then put a little glue on the top ends of the front and back pieces. While your helper gives you a hand, set the other side piece down on the gluey front and back pieces, fitting the bored holes over the dowels. You'll probably need to tap everything together with your hammer.

10. While your helper holds the corners of the assembly square, hammer a couple of 4d finishing nails into each joint so that the side is tight.

11. Now use your marking tools, clamp, and handsaw to measure, mark, and cut a base from a scrap of 1/4" plywood.

12. Set the assembly on your work surface with the sides on edge; the front and back should be 3/4" above the work surface. Run a line of glue around all four of the surfaces that are facing up, and set the base onto the gluey surfaces, carefully lining up all four corners.

13. With your hammer, drive No. 17 x 3/4" brads through the base and into all four pieces, spacing the brads a couple of inches apart.

14. Carefully sand the crumb box with 100-grit and then with 150-grit sandpaper. Wipe every bit of sawdust off when you're through, shaking the box vigorously to remove any dust from the inside.

15. Don't paint, stain, or varnish this project! These finishes have chemicals in them—ones you certainly wouldn't want to eat along with your bread! Instead, shine up your crumb box with a thin coat of mineral oil. Just put a few drops on a clean rag, and then rub the box well with the rag. Or ask your adult helper to select another safe finish for you. Remember, never put paint, stain, or varnish on any project that will come into contact with food.

16. Now surprise the house chef with your gift!

◈③ Cargo Ship

Ahoy there, barnacle-backs! Weigh anchor, and away all lines!

MATERIALS

1   Scrap 2 x 4, at least 28" long
1   Scrap 1 x 2, at least 10" long
1   Scrap 1" dowel, at least 12" long
1   1/2" dowel, 36" long
2   1/4" dowels, 36" long
1   Scrap 1-1/2" lattice, at least 16" long
    4d and 6d finishing nails
    Wood glue
    Sandpaper, 100-grit and 150-grit
    Masking tape
    A jar or can lid, about 4" in diameter
    A small piece of colorful plastic tape
    Varnish
    A stick for stirring
    Mineral spirits or turpentine
    1", 1/2", and detail paintbrushes
    Rags and newspapers

HINT!

If you plan to float your finished project in the bathtub or your local pond, be sure to get a waterproof varnish.

TOOLS

Marking tools	Hammer
C-clamp	Coping saw
Handsaw	Brace with 1/4" and 1" bit

CUT LIST

1	2 x 4 x 24"	Hull
1	2 x 4 x 3-1/2"	Cabin
1	1 x 2 x 3-1/2"	Bridge
3	1 x 2 x 2"	Boxes
4	4" x 1-1/2" lattice	Plywood
3	1" x 2" dowels	Smokestacks and winch
6	1" x 3/4" dowels	Barrels
9	4" x 1/2" dowels	Logs
2	1/4" x 16" dowels	Rails
2	1/4" x 3" dowels	Flag mast and foremast
1	1/4" x 2" dowel	Antenna

PUTTING IT TOGETHER

1. Use your marking tools, clamp, and handsaw to cut all the parts listed in the Cut List. (Use a coping saw to cut the thin dowel pieces.) To keep all these parts organized, stack and label them as you cut them. A miter box is a very helpful tool for cutting small parts. Consider building the one in "Part Three" if you haven't already!

2. Set the hull on edge on your work surface. On the top edge, near the hull's end, use your square and a pencil to draw an angled line, about 2-1/2" long. Use the photograph of the boy making this mark as a guide, but don't worry if your line doesn't match his exactly! You've just drawn the *bow* (or front) of your cargo ship.

3. Clamp the hull on its edge. Then, keeping the saw very straight, use your handsaw to cut right through the pencil line.

4. Now set the hull flat, with the cut part on the bottom. Use your tape measure and a pencil to mark the hull's center on the end of its top face, just above the cut you made. This mark should be at 1-3/4".

5. To make the rounded bow shape, use a jar or can lid as a pattern. Set the lid down on the hull's face so that its rounded edge touches your pencil mark and curves toward the back (or *stern*) of the ship. Mark along the lid with your pencil, on both sides of your marked center point.

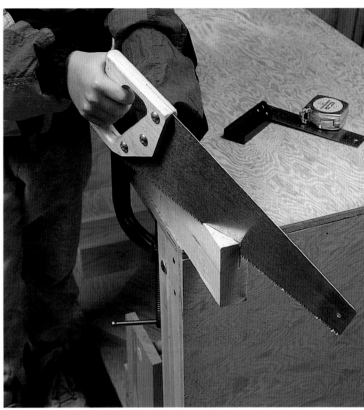

6. Clamp the hull down flat, and cut the two pencil lines with your coping saw.

7. Spread some glue on one face of the cabin, and set it on the hull's top face, with its front edge exactly 5" from the hull's stern end.

8. With your hammer, drive a couple of 6d finishing nails through the cabin, into the hull. Set these nails towards the cabin's bow end, because you'll soon be drilling holes at the stern end.

9. Using 4d nails, glue and nail the bridge to the cabin's top face, lining it up with the cabin's front edge.

10. Now you need to attach the two rails to the hull's top face. First, put a few dots of glue in several places along one side of each rail. Then set the rails carefully onto the deck so that they're parallel and 2-1/8" apart, and one end of each rail is tight against the cabin. Let the glue dry for an hour before you move your ship.

11. Tighten a 1/4" bit into your brace, and flag it with masking tape to bore a 1/2"-deep hole. Drill one 1/2"-deep hole (for the flag mast) on top of the bridge. Also drill two 1/2"-deep holes (for the foremast and antenna) on the deck; place these 1" apart and both within 2-1/2" of the bow. Use the photograph as a guide.

12. Put a drop or two of glue into each hole, and set the 1/4" flag mast, foremast, and antenna into the holes, tapping them with a hammer if necessary. The shorter antenna goes closest to the bow.

13. Replace the 1/4" bit in your brace with a 1" bit, and bore two holes, about 1/2" deep, in the cabin's top face, 1" behind the bridge and 3/4" apart from each other.

14. Glue and set the two smokestacks into the two holes.

15. Run a line of glue along one side of the winch. Set it carefully onto the deck just behind the cabin. Let the glue dry before moving the cargo ship.

16. Carefully sand your cargo ship and all its parts with 100-grit and 150-grit sandpaper. Remember to wipe the sawdust off.

17. Finish your ship with a couple of coats of varnish.

18. Make a flag by cutting a small piece of plastic tape and mounting it on your flag mast.

19. Load up your cargo ship, and show it to your friends and family!

ART & MUSIC

◈ Bull-Roarer

This mysterious music-maker will amaze your friends. Tell them the secret of its sound if they'd like to make bull-roarers for themselves!

MATERIALS

1   Scrap wood, 3/8" thick and at least 3-1/2" x 14", but not plywood

1   Scrap dowel, 6" long and at least 1/2" thick

     A metal fishing swivel, size 3 or larger

     Braided nylon cord, at least 6'

     Sandpaper, 100-grit and 150-grit

     Masking tape

     Exterior latex enamel paints, any color

     A stick for stirring

     1", 1/2", and detail paintbrushes

     Rags and newspapers

HINTS!

If you don't have a 3/8"-thick piece of scrap wood in your bin, try asking for one at a shop where cabinets and furniture are built. Take this book along when you do, and show the people there what you need; they may give you some scrap for free.

Buy your swivel from a fishing-supply salesperson; ask for help so that you get the right size.

Be sure to get braided cord; twisted cord will come apart when you spin your bull-roarer.

TOOLS

Marking tools   Handsaw

C-clamp   Brace with 1/4" bit

PUTTING IT TOGETHER

1. Using the illustration as a guide, use your marking tools to draw the shape of the bull-roarer onto your 3-1/2" x 14" scrap wood. Make your drawing as accurate as possible.

2. Clamp the scrap to your bench so that the drawing faces up, and cut out the shape with your handsaw. You'll need to turn the piece and re-clamp it before you saw each line.

3. Sand the bull-roarer that you've just cut.

4. Use your brace and a 1/4" bit to drill a small hole centered 1/2" from the longest pointed end of the bull-roarer.

5. Next, slip one end of a 4" piece of braided nylon cord through the hole.

6. Now slip the same cord end through one end of the swivel, and knot both ends of the cord together tightly.

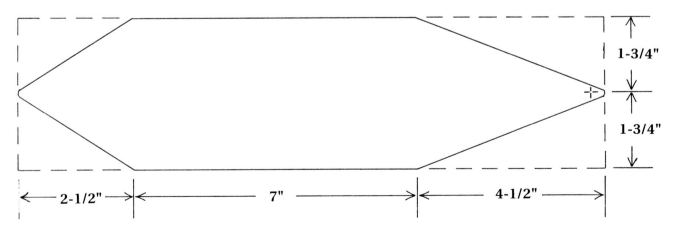

+ = hole location

1-3/4"

1-3/4"

2-1/2"   7"   4-1/2"

Magic on a String

The bull-roarer is an ancient instrument, which has been used for centuries by South Sea islanders and other native peoples in their ceremonies. When you swing your own bull-roarer and wonder at its sound, you're part of a timeless, worldwide musical tradition: the playing of handmade instruments.

This fascinating project makes its sound by creating vibrations in the air as it spins. The vibrations travel through the air until they reach you, where they tickle your inner ear and make what we call sound.

Take your project outside, well away from your friends. (An escaping bull-roarer is a dangerous beast!) Hold the dowel in your hand so that the cord comes out next to your middle finger. Swing the bull-roarer over your head, round and round. Experiment until you get the sound just right.

If your bull-roarer doesn't make a sound right away, first try swinging it in the other direction. Then try swinging it at different speeds. If it still doesn't work, check the swivel by holding it between two fingers and turning the bull-roarer with your other hand. If the wood can't turn freely on the swivel, replace the swivel.

Get your friends to make bull-roarers with you. Then spread out in a big yard or open field, and start your own bull-roarer orchestra!

7. Cut a 6" piece of dowel to make a handle. Then clamp the handle, with a piece of scrap wood underneath it, to your work surface. Next, use your brace and a 1/4" bit to bore a hole through the dowel, 3" from one end.

8. Now cut a 4' (or longer) piece of cord.

9. With a very tight knot, tie one end of this cord to the end of the swivel that doesn't have a cord through it yet.

10. Slip the other end of this longer piece of cord through the hole in the dowel, and tie it tightly. As you look at your assembled bull-roarer, you should see (in this order) a handle, long cord, swivel, short cord, and the bull-roarer. Tape the cord's ends to keep them from unravelling.

11. Paint your bull-roarer if you like. A really wild design with lots of colors will look great, but the choice is up to you!

 **Lively Snake**

Make your friends jump with this colorful snake,
or just let it curl up on your shelf!

MATERIALS

1   1 x 4 x 12" balsa wood, from a craft store
    Sandpaper, 150-grit
    Latex enamel paint, several colors
    A stick for stirring
    1/2" and detail paintbrushes
    Rags and newspapers

TOOLS

Marking tools   Coping saw
C-clamp   Rasp

PUTTING IT TOGETHER

1. Balsa wood is very soft and lightweight; it seems more like thick paper than like wood. Use your pencil to sketch a wiggly snake—almost 12" long and about 1" wide—on one face of the wood. Make the tail and head a little thinner than the body, but not so thin that they break. Balsa wood isn't very strong!

2. Clamp the wood to your work surface securely.

3. Then cut out the snake shape with a coping saw. Watch your fingers! If you can't reach part of the cutting line with your saw, just move the balsa wood and re-clamp it.

4. Use a rasp to shape the snake to your liking. Balsa gets a little fuzzy when you rasp it, but don't worry. The next step will take care of that.

5. Smooth the snake with a scrap of sandpaper, and wipe the sawdust off with a rag.

6. Now you're ready to paint your snake. First fill in a bright background with your 1/2" paintbrush and paints.

7. Once the background has dried, use your pencil to sketch any design that pleases you. Photographs of snakes in books about reptiles might give you some ideas. Remember to add the snake's eyes and mouth. Then use your detail paintbrushes to paint on the design.

8. After its painted "skin" has dried, place your snake on a display shelf, or put it where someone will find it. Watch to see how high that person jumps!

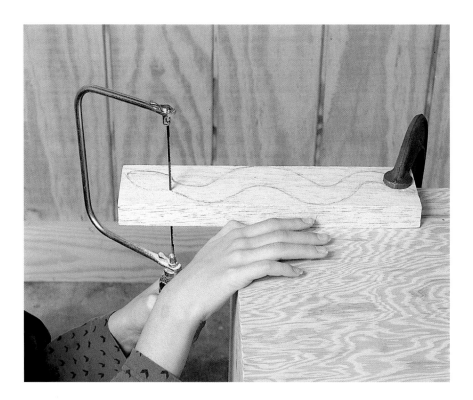

◈ Folk-Art Sculpture

Put your creativity on display!

MATERIALS

1 Scrap 1 x 8, at least 24" long
1 Scrap 1 x 4, at least 10" long
1 Scrap 1/4" plywood, about 6" x 6"
1 3/8" dowel, at least 12" long
   No. 17 x 3/4" brads
   3d finishing nails
   Sandpaper, 100-grit and 150-grit
   Wood glue
   Masking tape
   Exterior latex enamel paints,
      any colors
   A stick for stirring
   1" and detail paintbrushes
   Rags and newspapers

TOOLS

Marking tools   Hammer
C-clamp   Coping saw
Handsaw   Brace with 3/8" bit

CUT LIST

1 1 x 8 x 10"   Base
1 1 x 4 x 3-1/2"   Collar
1 3/8" dowel, 12" long   Rod
1 1 x 8 x 12"-14"   Cutout of a favorite
      plywood cutouts   animal: ears, a tail, etc.

PUTTING IT TOGETHER

1. Here's a chance to use your imagination! Think of an animal shape for your sculpture. Then, with your pencil, sketch the shape onto one end of the 1 x 8's face. Your animal should be stretched out, as if it's running (or, if it's a bird or fish, flying or swimming). Make the figure about 12" to 14" long, and longer than it is tall.

2. Clamp the 1 x 8 to your work surface, and cut out the shape with your coping saw, turning the figure and re-clamping it as necessary.

3. Now sketch the ears, wings, tail, or other details onto the 1/4" plywood. Make their size fit the animal shape's size; a giant pair of wings on a sparrow might look strange!

4. Clamp the plywood to your work surface, and cut out the detail pieces with your coping saw.

5. Use your marking tools, clamp, and handsaw to measure, mark, and cut the base, the collar, and the 12" dowel rod.

6. Find the collar's center by drawing two lines across its top face, from corner to corner. Use your hammer and a nail to dimple the center point, where the lines cross.

7. Clamp the collar to your work surface with a scrap of wood sandwiched between the two, and use your brace and a 3/8" bit to bore a hole through the dimpled mark, right through the collar.

8. Spread some glue on the collar's face. Then set it in the center of the base's face. (Use your eyes to guess where the base's center is, and then use your tape measure to check that the collar is centered correctly.)

9. Hammer four 3d finishing nails into the collar's face, one through each corner.

10. Put a little glue into the assembly's hole. Then push or tap one end of the rod into the hole, and set the assembly aside to dry.

11. Clamp the animal figure upside down to the edge of your work surface. With your tape measure and pencil, measure from one of its ends, and mark the center of the edge that's on top (which is really the bottom of the figure). The mark will probably be on the belly of your cutout, but this center mark doesn't have to be exact.

12. Use your brace and a 3/8" bit flagged for boring a 1"-deep hole to drill a really straight hole into the mark you made.

13. Carefully sand all parts of the animal figure with 100-grit and 150-grit sandpaper, and wipe the sawdust off. Also sand the base-and-collar assembly.

14. Now glue and nail the detail parts to the main figure. (Use brads for this nailing job.)

15. Put a little glue into the hole on the animal figure, and then push or tap the figure down onto the rod's top end. Turn the figure so that it lines up with the base's long grain, and set the assembly aside to dry.

16. Paint your folk-art sculpture any way you like, and sign your name on its base. Then give it to someone who will show it off!

Whistle

This tooter is terrific!

MATERIALS

1 Scrap 1 x 2, at least 5" long
1 Scrap 3/8" dowel, at least 12" long
   Wood glue
   Sandpaper, 100-grit
   Thin, colored cord, about 30" long

TOOLS

Marking tools	Hammer
C-clamp	Coping saw
Handsaw	Brace with 1/4" and 3/8" bits

CUT LIST

1 1 x 2 x 5"   Whistle
2 3/8" dowels, each 1" long   Dowels
   (Read the instructions before you cut these angled pieces!)

3/4"   3/4"

1-1/4"

1"

x = hole location

Dowels (2)

3/8"

3/8"

7/16"

PUTTING IT TOGETHER

1. Use your marking tools, clamp, and handsaw to cut a piece of 1 x 2, exactly 5" long.

2. Clamp this piece (the whistle) to your work surface with one end straight up.

3. Using your marking tools, and the illustration as a guide, mark the whistle's top end.

4. Dimple the two marks with your hammer and a nail.

5. With your brace and a flagged 3/8" bit, bore a 2-1/4"-deep hole straight down through one of the dimpled marks. Then change the masking tape flag to 3-1/4", and bore a hole of that depth down through the other dimpled mark. (It doesn't matter which hole gets

bored at which mark.) Hold the brace and bit very straight, or the bit will bore out the side of the 1 x 2. If this happens, read "Foozles and Flumadiddles" on page 57 before you go back to Step 1!

6. Set the whistle flat on your work surface, and use your marking tools to square a line across the top face, 1" from the end with the holes in it. Then, measuring from the piece's top face, mark 3/8" down on each edge, just below each end of the line that you drew.

7. Clamp the whistle to your work surface. With your handsaw, make a 3/8"-deep cut into the 1" line. Stop sawing as soon as the blade touches the two edge marks you made! If you've built a miter box, use it instead of a clamp to hold the work as you cut.

8. Now use your marking tools to square another line across the top face, 2-1/4" from the end with the holes in it.

9. Get a hand from your adult helper with the next couple of steps. Turn the whistle on one edge. Using your pencil and a small, straight scrap of wood as a ruler, connect the end of the line that you just drew with the bottom of the 3/8" cut. Then turn the piece over onto its other edge, and do the same thing. You've now marked an angled line on each of the whistle's edges.

10. Clamp the whistle upright to your work surface, with the holes on the bottom and the cut facing you. Have your helper give you a hand starting the blade of your coping saw at an angle into the 2-1/4" line, and then saw down the angled line until you reach the bottom of the 3/8"-deep cut. Check both edges as you cut to make sure that you're following the lines on both of them. When you're finished, a small, angled

piece of scrap should fall out. If it doesn't, get some help sawing or wiggling it loose.

11. Now clamp the 3/8" dowel upright onto your work surface so that about 2" of dowel is above the clamp. Use your pencil and tape measure to make a small mark on the dowel's side, 1" down from its top end.

12. Next, have an adult helper start your coping saw blade down into the top end of the dowel, with the blade centered exactly half-way across it. Now, as you cut, angle the blade toward the mark you made so that the blade cuts out through the dowel right at the 1" mark, leaving a sharp edge on the piece you cut. Set the little angled piece aside in a safe place.

13. Put the long dowel flat on your work surface or in a miter box, and cut a square end on it.

14. Now repeat Steps 11 and 12 to cut another 1"-long angled dowel piece. Set it aside with the other one.

15. Put a small drop of glue onto the rounded edge of one of the 1"-long angled dowel pieces (not on the angled edge), and slide or tap it into one of the holes in the whistle. Put in the large end of the gluey piece first, and make sure its flat top faces up towards the whistle's top face. Push it in so that the small end of the gluey piece is even with the whistle's end, and the rounded bottom edge of the dowel piece is tight against the round side of the hole.

Use a large nail to adjust the dowel piece until it fits just right.

16. Repeat Step 15 to glue and position the other 1" piece into the other hole. Then carefully wipe off any drops of glue, and set your whistle aside until the glue dries.

17. Clamp the whistle to your work surface with a piece of scrap sandwiched between them, and use your marking tools to measure and mark an X on the top face, 3/4" from the end without the holes, and 3/4" from one edge.

18. Use your brace and a 1/4" bit to bore a hole through the X.

19. Carefully sand your whistle with 100-grit sandpaper, wipe the sawdust off, and slip and knot the cord through the 1/4" hole.

20. Try blowing hard through your whistle, putting your mouth over both holes at once. If the sound isn't very clear, shake your whistle, or tap it on your work surface to remove any sawdust from the blow holes. If you made the angled cuts in the two dowel pieces correctly and carefully followed the instructions for boring and sawing the 5" piece, your whistle should wake up dogs and cats all over the neighborhood!

Leaf Mobile

This mobile, made from balsa wood, is just as easy on the eyes as it is to make.

MATERIALS

1   1/4" x 3-1/2" x 24" balsa wood
1   1/8" dowel, at least 20" long
     A push pin or a No. 17 x 3/4" brad
     Wood glue
     Sandpaper, 150-grit
     Leaves
     Straight pins
     Light-colored sewing thread
     Latex enamel paint, autumn or summer leaf colors
     A stick for stirring
     1/2" and detail paintbrushes
     Rags and newspapers

HINT!

You can get balsa wood from a crafts or hobby shop.

TOOLS

     Marking tools
     C-clamp
     Coping saw

PUTTING IT TOGETHER

1. First, find some leaves with shapes that you like. The mobile in the photograph was inspired by colorful autumn leaves, but you can just as easily use fresh green leaves for a bright, summery mobile instead. Make as many leaf shapes for your mobile as you like; just remember that the more leaves you make, the more difficult it will be to get the mobile to balance properly.

2. Set your leaves flat on the balsa wood, and trace around them with a pencil. Add a wide, 1/2"-long stem to each leaf shape.

3. Clamp the balsa wood to your work surface, and then carefully cut out the leaf shapes with your coping saw. You'll notice right away that the blade slips through the soft balsa wood very easily, so use a light touch when you're sawing! Loosen the handle, and turn the saw blade whenever you need to in order to stay on the line.

4. To smooth the leaf shapes' edges, sand them lightly with 150-grit sandpaper.

5. With your measuring tape, pencil, and coping saw, measure, mark, and cut one 12" and one 8" piece of 1/8" dowel. Sand their ends lightly, and wipe away any sawdust.

6. Next, paint the leaf shapes in any colors you like. Paint one side at a time, letting the first side dry

before you turn the shape over to paint the other side. Paint the edges too!

7. When the leaf shapes have dried completely, push a straight pin almost all the way into the end of each stem. Also push a straight pin almost all the way into the bottom edge of one of the biggest leaf shapes. You'll use this big leaf as the mobile's center leaf.

8. Arrange your leaves on a flat surface with the dowels placed in the positions they'll be in when the mobile is hanging. (The 12" dowel hangs above the 8" dowel.) Get an adult friend to help you arrange all the parts so that they won't get tangled when the mobile twists in the air.

9. Next, tie a 10" piece of thread onto each stem's pin, and then tie the other end onto the dowels. You'll notice in the photograph that the bottom leaf is tied to the pin below the large center leaf. Try to make the leaves hang at slightly different lengths, and cut off the extra thread after you've tied each knot.

10. Then tie a piece of thread onto the center of the 12" dowel. Make the thread long enough to suspend your mobile from a window, ceiling, or doorway. Hang up the mobile with a push pin or a brad, and adjust the balance of each leaf shape by gently sliding the thread knots along the two dowels until all the parts hang evenly.

11. Put a small drop of white glue onto each knot; when the glue dries, it will hold the knots tightly in place.

12. Now watch your mobile turn gently in the breeze!

Art & Music 151

 Slit Drum

Here's a box with a beat!

MATERIALS

1 Scrap 1 x 8, at least 28" long
1 Scrap 1 x 6, at least 40" long
1 Scrap 1/4" dowel, at least 24" long
2 Small, hard rubber "superballs"
4 Cleats, rubber or plastic, that attach with nails or screws
   4d finishing nails
   Wood glue
   Epoxy glue
   Sandpaper, 100-grit and 150-grit
   Masking tape
   Varnish
   A stick for stirring
   Mineral spirits or turpentine
   1" paintbrush
   Rags and newspapers

TOOLS

Marking tools	Coping saw
C-clamp	Brace with 1/4" and 3/8" bit
Handsaw	Rasp
Hammer	

CUT LIST

2	1 x 6 x 14"	Side panels
2	1 x 8 x 14"	Bottom and top
2	1 x 6, each about 6" long, depending on the width of the 1 x 8	End panels
2	1/4" dowel, each 12" long	Beater sticks

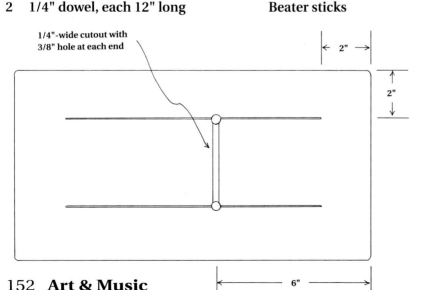

1/4"-wide cutout with 3/8" hole at each end

2"

2"

6"

PUTTING IT TOGETHER

1. Using your marking tools, clamp, and handsaw, cut two 14"-long side panels from the 1 x 6 and two 14"-long pieces (a top and a bottom) from the 1 x 8.

2. Have a friend hold one side panel on one long edge. Then put a thin line of glue along its top edge.

3. Now place the bottom piece on top of the side panel's edge so that the bottom's edge lines up with the side panel's face. Hammer several 4d finishing nails through the bottom's face, each about 3/8" from the edge.

4. Repeat Steps 2-3 with the other side panel and the pieces you just nailed together, lining up the other side panel just as you lined up the first one, but placing it on the other side of the bottom's face.

5. Turn the nailed assembly over so that the bottom rests flat on your work surface.

6. At either end of the assembly, measure the distance between the inside faces of the side panels.

7. Using your marking tools and handsaw, cut two 1 x 6 end panels to the length you just measured.

8. Run a thin line of glue along the three inside faces at one end of the assembly, about 3/8" from the ends. Slip one of the end panels into the end of the assembly, right where you've applied the glue. Make sure that the end panel's face lines up with the

ends of the assembly. Then have a friend hold the assembly while you secure the end panel by hammering 4d finishing nails into each side panel and into the bottom.

9. Repeat Step 8 to glue and nail up the other end panel. Set the assembly aside while the glue dries.

10. Next, find the 1 x 8 x 14" top. Using the illustration as a guide, mark the slits on this piece. The marked shape looks a bit like the letter H, doesn't it?

11. Clamp the top, with some scrap wood under it, to your work surface. Now use your brace and a 3/8" bit to bore two holes right

through the top, at the points where the H's center line touches the H's two sides.

12. Use your coping saw to start the cuts in the holes you drilled. Continue the cuts down each of the three lines.

Dig That Crazy Rhythm

The slit drum is a popular instrument; its bubbly sounds are enjoyed by people around the world. When you strike your drum's tongues with your beaters, the air inside the drum vibrates and then escapes through the slits in the drum's top.

You may have noticed that the two tongues on your drum are of different lengths. The tone a tongue produces depends on how big the tongue is compared with the size of the drum; larger tongues move more air when they're struck with the beater. Even a slight difference in length (say 1/4") will make a tongue's tone higher or lower. With a little care and creativity, you can give a slit drum more "voices" (more different tones) by cutting out four or more tongues of varying lengths. The tongues shouldn't be cut thinner than 1", however. Experiment with your slit drum, and you'll find that there are many different sounds and rhythms at your fingertips.

21. Finish off your slit drum with two coats of varnish, letting each coat dry well.

22. Attach one floor cleat to each bottom corner of your slit drum.

Quiet!

If your indoor drumming is driving other people to distraction, you can soften the sound your beaters make by covering them with felt.

MATERIALS

2   Superball beaters
4   Scraps of felt
    A jar lid, over 3" in diameter
    A pair of wire-cutting pliers
    Scissors
    Thin (16-gauge) copper, aluminum, or steel wire

13. Next, make the center cut of the H (the short line that connects the two long lines) 1/4" wider than the other two cuts by making a second saw-cut close to the first one. This wide opening will let the sound in the drum reach your ears.

14. Run a thin line of glue along all four top edges of the assembly.

15. Set the top on the glued edges, lining it up carefully, and securing it by hammering in evenly spaced 4d finishing nails, just as you nailed the bottom.

16. With your marking tools and coping saw, cut two 12" dowel beater sticks.

17. Rest one of your C-clamps flat on the work surface, and then tighten a superball into the clamp.

18. Next, flag a 1/4" bit with a piece of masking tape wrapped exactly 1/2" above the bit's cutters (not above the bit's screw-tip). Have a helper hold the clamped superball firmly while you use your brace and the flagged 1/4" bit to bore a 1/2"-deep hole into the center of the superball. Bore a hole in the other superball, too.

19. Mix a small amount of epoxy glue, following the directions on the container. With a small scrap of wood, put a little glue into the hole in a superball, and then push a beater stick all the way into the hole. Repeat this step with the other beater stick and superball. You've just made two beaters!

20. Round the edges of the drum with a rasp, and then sand all parts of the drum really well. A folded piece of sandpaper is perfect for smoothing the inside edges of the slits on the top. Sand the beater handles, too.

1. Set the jar lid on the felt, and trace around its edges with a pen or pencil.

2. Cut out the traced circle with your scissors. Trace and cut out three more circles of the same size.

3. Use your pliers to cut two 4"-long pieces of wire.

4. Lay one felt circle on top of another, and then wrap the double layer tightly over the superball at the end of the beater.

5. Wrap a piece of wire tightly around the felt, just below the superball. Twist the ends of the wire together, and then wrap this twisted wire closely around the beater stick, over the felt. Repeat Step 1-4 with two more felt circles and the second beater.

6. A whomp-bompaloobomp, a bim-bam-BOOM!

◆③ **Puppet Theater**

Ladies and gentlemen! Let the show begin!

MATERIALS

1 4' x 8' paint-grade plywood, 3/8" or 1/2" thick
1 Scrap 1 x 4, at least 48" long
3 Pairs 1-1/2" x 1-1/2" leaf hinges with screws
   3d and 4d finishing nails
   Wood glue
   Sandpaper, 100-grit and 150-grit
   Latex enamel paint, in colors you like
   A stick for stirring
   1" and 1/2" paintbrushes
   Rags and newspapers

HINTS!

See Step 1 before you buy the plywood.

If you can't find leaf hinges, strap hinges will do.

To save some time on this big project, borrow a larger paintbrush than the ones listed above.

To saw out the opening in the front of the puppet theater, you'll need to borrow a special saw, called a keyhole saw. If you can't find one, have an adult helper cut out the opening with a power tool called a jigsaw.

To drive the small screws into the hinges, you may also need a smaller screwdriver than your No. 2. Your adult helper can give you a hand.

If the points of any screws or nails poke out the front or sides, ask your adult helper to blunt them with a file or hammer so that they don't cut your fingers.

This is a good project to work on with your adult helper. You can follow the directions together!

TOOLS

Keyhole saw or jigsaw	Hammer
Marking tools	Screwdriver
C-clamp	Coping saw
Handsaw	Brace with 1" bit

CUT LIST

1	36" x 48" plywood, 3/8" or 1/2" thick	Front
3	20" x 48" plywood, 3/8" or 1/2" thick	Sides and back
2	1 x 4 x 24"	Stage pieces

PUTTING IT TOGETHER

1. Begin by having someone at the lumberyard saw your plywood into the four pieces listed in the Cut List. Three cuts should be made, each one across the plywood's width, not along its length.

2. Set the front piece on your work surface. Then take a good look at the illustration. Next, use your marking tools and a straight scrap of wood (at least 36" long) to mark the three straight sides of the stage opening. Have your adult helper give you a hand when you mark the curved line.

3. Now use your brace and a 1" bit to drill a hole just inside each corner of the marked line. Remember to clamp a bit of scrap wood under the plywood to keep your drill bit from ruining your work surface.

4. Set the plywood on your work surface so that you can cut out one part of the marked line at a time, moving the plywood as necessary. Your helper can show you how to use the keyhole saw. To start, hold the handle firmly, set the point of the saw into one of the four holes you drilled, and begin sawing along a marked line. For the straight lines, start a cut about 5" long with the keyhole saw, and then continue sawing the line with your handsaw, which cuts straight lines much better. For the curved line, use the keyhole saw; cutting lines like these is its favorite job! Continue cutting until the marked piece falls out.

5. Now set the 1 x 4 on your work surface, and use your marking tools, clamp, and handsaw to measure, clamp, and cut two stage pieces, each 24" long.

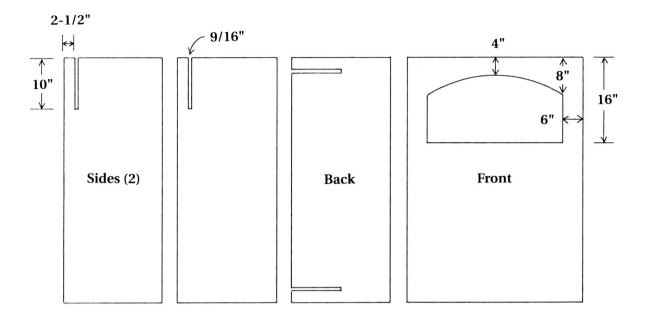

6. Next, set the front on the work surface with the side that you want to paint facing up. Run a couple of glue lines along one face of a stage piece, and put the gluey face onto the front's face, lining up the stage piece's top edge with the bottom edge of the front's opening. Line up the stage piece's ends with the bottom corners of the opening, too.

7. Use your hammer to drive 3d finishing nails through the stage piece and into the front, spacing the nails about 4" apart.

8. Now set the front upright on the ground, and have your helper steady it. Run a line of glue along the top edge of the stage piece that you just nailed in place. Then set the other stage piece flat on top of the glue line so that one of its long edges is even with the back (inside) face of the front.

9. Hammer 4d finishing nails through the face of the stage piece that you just glued in place, into the other stage piece. Be careful not to hammer these nails into the front. (If you need to, you

can use your tape measure to check where the nails should go. They should be driven about 3/4" from the top stage piece's inside edge. Space the nails about 5" apart.

10. Set a 20" x 48" side flat on your work surface. Measure and mark it so that it looks just like the side in the illustration. (The slots are 9/16" wide; measure and mark carefully!)

11. Use your handsaw to make the 10"-long cuts. Then use your coping saw to cut the end of the plywood "tongue" off at the end of the 10" cuts.

12. Repeat Steps 10 and 11 to measure, mark, and cut the tongue from the second side piece.

13. Next, set the 20" x 48" back flat on your work surface, and measure and mark the two slots in it. These slots are the same size as those in the sides and the same distance from the edge, but there are two of them instead of one!

14. Saw out these two tongues with your handsaw and coping saw.

15. Set the front flat on the floor or ground, with the stage pieces facing down. Using your screwdriver, attach three hinges near each edge of the front piece's back face. Your adult helper or someone at the hardware store can show you how these hinges are put on. Space the hinges about 20" apart from one another.

16. Now have your helper hold the edge of a side piece tight against the hinges, so that the side and front line up. (Make sure that the 10"-long cutouts and the stage cutout are all at the same end, and that the side's face that you intend to paint is facing down.) Connect the side and front to one another by using your screwdriver to attach the hinges to the side.

17. Repeat Step 16 to attach the other side to the front.

18. Set the puppet theater upright, and fold the two sides back so that they're almost at right angles to the front. Then slip the two cutouts in the back down into the cutouts in the sides.

19. Using 100-grit and 150-grit sandpaper, sand the theater really well. Watch out for splinters!

20. Paint your puppet theater any way you like; the more imaginative you can be, the better!

Puppet Theater Curtain

MATERIALS

1   3/8" dowel, 36" long
2   1-7/16" (medium) screw eyes
1   Square yard of velvety red cloth
    A sewing needle and some thread
1   Yard of braided rope, also velvety to the touch
    Cellophane tape

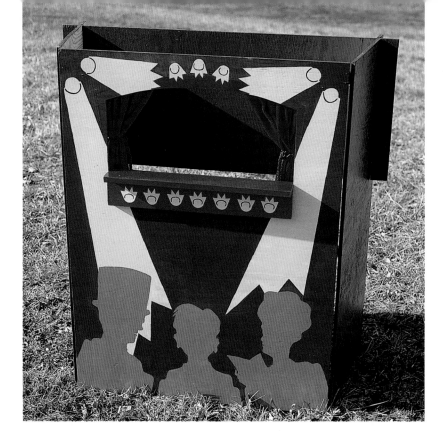

1. Use your hammer to start the point of a screw eye into the front's back face, just above the stage opening that you cut out. Use your fingers or the shaft of your screwdriver to tighten the screw eye into the plywood. Then fasten the other screw eye just above the opening's other top corner. (Be sure that the two screw eyes are lined up with one another.)

2. Use a pair of scissors to cut the red cloth along one edge so that it measures 20" x 36".

3. To make a tube shape in the cloth (for the dowel curtain-

hanger), fold one edge of the cloth over about 1-1/2", and sew the bottom edge of the fold. Do get some help with the sewing if you need it.

4. Now cut the curtain in half, right across the fold.

5. Push the 3/8" dowel through both folds. Bunch the curtains up in the middle of the dowel so that you can slip the dowel's ends through the screw eyes. To open or close the curtains, just slide them along the dowel.

6. Cut the braided rope, and tape its ends so that they don't unravel. Then use a piece of rope to tie each curtain open.

Acknowledgements & Metric Equivalency Chart

Thanks to everyone who provided ideas, photographs, and locations for photography. Also thanks to The Louisville Slugger, Louisville, KY. And special thanks to the kids, who enthusiastically measured, sawed, and hammered their way through the building of *Woodworking for Kids!*

ADDITIONAL PHOTOGRAPHY

Page 10

Logging
Courtesy Rick Odum
Haywood Community College, Clyde, NC

Page 6

Daimler Riding Car
Bild-Nr. 59720
Courtesy German Information Center, New York, NY

LOCATION PHOTOGRAPHY

Pat and Roger McGuire, Swan Mountain Farm, Asheville, NC

Anne Kelley McGuire, Asheville, NC

Westall & Johnson Chandley Lumber Co., Inc., Asheville, NC

THE KIDS

Douglas Ager, Anna and Mary Bracken, Yannick and Yuri Brewster, Phelps Clark, Mark Eaton deVerges, Laurel and Morgan Fender, Anna and Jeff Jacobson, Patrick and Matthew McGuire, Molly McGuire, Imari and Levonda Norman, Austin Sconyers-Snow, Adrian, Christopher, and Hillary Sherman

Metric Equivalency Chart

LINEAR

Inches	CM	Inches	CM
1/8	0.3	25	63.5
1/4	0.6	26	66.0
3/8	1.0	27	68.6
1/2	1.3	28	71.1
5/8	1.6	29	73.7
3/4	1.9	30	76.2
7/8	2.2	31	78.7
1	2.5	32	81.3
1-1/4	3.2	33	83.8
1-1/2	3.8	34	86.4
1-3/4	4.4	35	88.9
2	5.1	36	91.4
2-1/2	6.4	37	94.0
3	7.6	38	96.5
3-1/2	8.9	39	99.1
4	10.2	40	101.6
4-1/2	11.4	41	104.1
5	12.7	42	106.7
6	15.2	43	109.2
7	17.8	44	111.8
8	20.3	45	114.3
9	22.9	46	116.8
10	25.4	47	119.4
11	27.9	48	121.9
12	30.5	49	124.5
13	33.0	50	127.0
14	35.6		
15	38.1		
16	40.6		
17	43.2		
18	45.7		
19	48.3		
20	50.8		
21	53.3		
22	55.9		
23	58.4		
24	61.0		

CAPACITY
1 pint = .473 litres
1 quart = .946 litres
1 gallon = 3.785 litres

WEIGHT
1 ounce = 28.35 grams
1 pound = 453.6 grams

Index